YOUR KNOWLEDGE HAS VALUE

AF136319

- We will publish your bachelor's and master's thesis, essays and papers

- Your own eBook and book - sold worldwide in all relevant shops

- Earn money with each sale

Upload your text at www.GRIN.com
and publish for free

Bibliographic information published by the German National Library:

The German National Library lists this publication in the National Bibliography; detailed bibliographic data are available on the Internet at http://dnb.dnb.de .

Cover image: wikipedia.org

Imprint:

Copyright © 2020 GRIN Verlag
Print and binding: Books on Demand GmbH, Norderstedt Germany
ISBN: 9783346174468

This book at GRIN:

https://www.grin.com/document/704282

Thorsten Prill, Johann van Wyk

The Namibian Church and Money

A Biblical Perspective

GRIN Verlag

GRIN - Your knowledge has value

Since its foundation in 1998, GRIN has specialized in publishing academic texts by students, college teachers and other academics as e-book and printed book. The website www.grin.com is an ideal platform for presenting term papers, final papers, scientific essays, dissertations and specialist books.

Visit us on the internet:

http://www.grin.com/

http://www.facebook.com/grincom

http://www.twitter.com/grin_com

The Namibian Church and Money

A Biblical Perspective

Johann van Wyk

Thorsten Prill

Namibian Theological Research Papers

Volume 2

Series Editor: Thorsten Prill

Dedication

We dedicate this book to all members of the Rhenish Church in Namibia.

Each of you should give what you have decided in your heart to give, not reluctantly or under compulsion, for God loves a cheerful giver. (2 Corinthians 9:7)

Acknowledgements

We are very grateful to Daan van der Kraan, Kathleen Demircan and Ryan Peter McKernan for their helpful comments and corrections.

Johann van Wyk & Thorsten Prill

Windhoek & Edinburgh, May 2020

Contents

Foreword

Money can be a hot topic in Christian churches and the Namibian church is no exception to that. While many traditional mainline denominations struggle to raise the funds they need for their various ministries, prosperity type churches and Pentecostal church bodies seem to flourish financially in Namibia. Some people are quick to point out that the main reason for this phenomenon lies in the churches' differing attitude towards the concept of tithing. While tithing plays a central role in Pentecostal and prosperity churches, most Protestant denominations rely on other ways of funding. In his paper, Thorsten Prill gives a critical overview of the various methods Namibian churches use to raise funds. These methods include collections, membership fees, fundraising events, commercial activities and investment trusts as well as encouraging members to give a tenth of the income to the church. In a second paper, Johann van Wyk examines the concept of tithing from a biblical perspective. He demonstrates that New Testament teachings do not support the claim that Christians are obliged to tithe. There are, however, a number of helpful biblical principles of giving which Namibian churches should apply. Most importantly, van Wyk argues, that giving in Namibian churches needs to become a matter of the heart; giving must be driven by love and grace.

Blessing Chishanu

Bristol, May 2020

Namibian Churches and Funding: A Critical Introduction

Thorsten Prill

Introduction

Today, about 80 to 90 percent of Namibia's multicultural population of 2.5 million is affiliated to a church (CIA 2020). The majority of them belong to churches of the Lutheran tradition (Tonchi et.al 2012:57-58). There are, however, other denominational groups, such as Anglicans, Baptists, Methodists, African Methodist Episcopalians, Charismatics, Pentecostals, Roman Catholics, and Reformed Christians (:57-58), as well as an increasing number of African Initiated Churches and Christian sects (cf. Tjimbundu 2018). The Christian Church has played a prominent role in the history of Namibia and is still a visible and important part of Namibian society today or, as Anene Ejikeme (2011:43) puts it: 'Christianity has deeply affected all strata of contemporary Namibian life, whether in rural or urban areas, in elite suburbs or poor neighbourhoods.' Since they receive no funding from the state and very little support from international church partners, as in most parts of the world, Namibian churches have to raise the money they need to finance their ministries. The methods Namibian churches use to raise funds can differ significantly.

Collections, Membership Fees and Fundraising Campaigns

In 2012, *The Namibian*, Namibia's largest daily newspaper, reported that the financial situation of Namibia's largest Christian denomination, the Evangelical Lutheran Church in Namibia (ELCIN), had reached crisis point. The church was N$2 million in debt (Shivute 2012). Since the country's independence from South Africa in 1990 funding from Finnish and other Western churches and parachurch organisations had continually ebbed away. As a result, ELCIN was struggling to fulfil her financial obligations and decided to have 'a fundraising campaign to collect as much money as possible from members' (Shivute 2012). Such

1

fundraising campaigns have become a common feature in the life of Namibian churches and para-church organisations.

Many Namibian church bodies, especially mainline denominations, rely not only on membership fees, gifts, and collections taken in the Sunday services (cf. Nangula 2013:57), but also on fundraising activities, such as church bazaars, potjiekos competitions, gala dinners, or the sale of braaivleis (grilled meat) or lottery tickets, to meet their financial needs. These methods of financing ministry may be helpful but they are not without challenges. While gala dinners, for example, might be an easy and effective way of generating extra income for a congregation, they tend to exclude less affluent church members who cannot afford to pay N$750 or more for a three-course meal in an upmarket hotel or lodge.

Likewise, a system of fixed membership fees can be problematic. In some Namibian churches the failure to pay membership fees can have far-reaching consequences. Non paying members might thus be denied their voting rights in church affairs, disqualified from holding a church office or suspended from enjoying other privileges (cf. ELCRN 2009:12). It is not uncommon that church members are told that a new-born child cannot be baptised or a deceased family member cannot be buried in the church cemetery because the family membership fees are in arrears. Failure to 'bring regularly all contributions and offerings which have been decided upon by the Church', as stipulated by the constitution of the Evangelical Lutheran Church in the Republic of Namibia (ELCRN 2009:11), is considered a serious offence.

In many Western cultures, Christians are encouraged to make a lasting gift by leaving a legacy to their church (cf. O'Neill 1999:101). Helen Cameron (2010:67) writes the following about such gifts: 'Legacies are invested in catch-up repairs to buildings or the purchase of an item (such as an organ) that would require extensive fundraising otherwise.' In Namibia, this practice is more or less unknown. The main reason being that the inheritance systems of the various Namibian ethnic groups guarantee that traditional offices, rights and material wealth, such as land, livestock, and personal belongings, stay in the maternal and/or paternal family of the deceased (cf. Bollig 2007:198). In many Ovambo cultures, for example, the traditional custom of matrilineal inheritance means that upon a man's death his wife does not inherit from him since she does not belong to his clan (cf. Lebert 2005:75). Instead, possessions are reclaimed by his maternal family (: 84).

Likewise, significant one-off donations to Namibian churches tend to be a rarity. So rare, in fact, they are considered worthy of coverage in the national press. Thus, in September 2018, *The Namibian*, for example, reported the following about such a donation:

> Prominent businessman Johannes !Gawaxab donated half-a-million dollars towards the construction of the Ebenezer Evangelical Lutheran Church at Mariental a week ago [...] The construction, estimated to cost N$6,5 million, will be completed in the first week of September 2019. !Gawaxab, who is also the project's patron and his wife, Paulina, offered to pay half of the construction's costs. "The new church will triple the capacity of our beloved church at Mariental due to the growth of the congregation over the last 80 years," !Gawaxab said.

Commercial Activities

Some Namibian churches receive extra income by renting out church premises, organising hospitality events or offering leadership conferences and workshops for which they charge commercial rates. So far, income from such activities has been exempted from income tax. In 2018, however, the Namibian government announced plans to tax income made by churches and charities from any business activities. In October 2019, Tonateni Shidhudhu (quoted by Kambowe 2019), spokesperson of the Ministry of Finance, explained the government's plans:

> Churches will be required to declare and pay tax on income received from commercial activities such as property rental, hospitality industry, transport industry and other types of income derived from activities of a commercial nature. It is anticipated that religious, educational and charitable institutions will be taxed at the current tax rate of 32%.

The government stressed that their decision would enhance the fairness of the tax system (Kambowe 2019). Churches were assured that income derived from membership fees, donations, etc., would continue to be tax-free. Ludwig Beukes, general secretary of the Council of Churches, expressed his doubts about the effectiveness of this new policy. In an interview, he said that 'it remains to be seen if [the] Inland Revenue will manage to get its way in collecting significantly from the already struggling churches' (Chiringa 2018).

Investment Trusts

To generate additional income some mainline Namibian denominations, such as the Evangelical Lutheran Church in Namibia (ELCIN), the Evangelical Lutheran Church in the Republic of Namibia (ELCRN) and the Rhenish Church in Namibia, have established for-profit investment trusts.[1] These trusts or business arms, which are legal entities in their own right and which operate independently of the church leadership, invest money in various business activities and transfer the profit they make to the respective church. The ELCRN Business Trust, for example, manages several conference centres and guesthouses to create extra revenue for the second-largest Protestant church in the country (World Council of Churches 2020).

The idea of business activities financing Christian ministries is not a new one. The apostle Paul, for example, worked as a tentmaker to support his evangelistic work (cf. Acts 18:3). He deliberately waived his right to receive a benefice from the Christian communities among whom he served (1 Cor. 9:15). Paul chose to do so because he did not want to be a burden to the church (1 Thes. 2:9; 2 Thes. 3:7-8).

For Namibian churches that want to go down that route, the challenge is to raise enough seed capital and make sure that each investment is socially responsible and in line with agreed ethical standards (e.g. no immoral activities, high standards of employee welfare, respect for the dignity and sanctity of human life etc.). The socio-economic conditions in Namibia present another challenge. In a

---

[1] The establishment of business arms is recommended by the Lutheran Community in Southern Africa (LUCSA) of which ELCIN is a member. See LUCSA, *Strategy 2013-2017: A Work in Progress*, 11. http://www.elcz.co.zw/uploads/1/1/4/0/11402736/lucsa_2013-2017_strategic_plan.pdf; Date of access: 18.04.2020.

country with an unemployment rate of over thirty percent and one of the highest levels of income inequality in the world (World Bank 2019), only larger denominations or churches that serve the more affluent segments of Namibian society will be able to launch their own business trusts. Smaller churches whose members belong to the forty percent of the population which are 'classified as multi-dimensionally poor' (Melber 2020) will need to cooperate with other church bodies if they want to benefit from an investment trust.

Recognising that many Namibian churches are lacking sufficient income, Martin Mwinga (2012), a Namibian economist, suggests that churches should set up one common trust under the umbrella of the Namibian Council of Churches to raise funds for socio-economic projects, such as Aids programmes or health facilities. In a research paper he writes:

> We recommend the establishment of a Christian Investment Fund to be owned by all participating churches in Namibia. One of the challenges faced by many churches in undertaking socio-economic projects is lack of capital to finance projects. Traditionally churches in Namibia raise capital through tithes and offerings by church members and sometimes these are not enough to cover both operational and capital budget of the church. We recommend that the Church use their limited resources and undertake leveraged investments to generate more income for the church. To this end we recommend that the Church collectively establish a Christian investment fund that will be used as an investment vehicle by churches, individuals, and other investors such as pension funds, companies and international organizations (:27).

Tithing and the Prosperity Gospel

In other Namibian church circles tithing is a widely accepted practice. Christians are asked to give ten percent of their income to their church. However, tithing is also a practice that has received sharp criticism. In 2018, the Namibian online magazine *The Villager*, for example, published an article entitled 'Beware of Greedy Pastors'. In this article, tithing is presented as the favourite doctrine of a certain type of church leader:

This is the big daddy. This is their sacred cow. This is the beating heart of their evil empire. The crown jewel. The Death Star. The one ring to bill them all. The pot of gold. Their matrix (into which they want to plug you). The Wizzard of Oz. Their magic spell. The special power. Their secret recipe with the elven herbs and spices. Their Golden Goose. The very air upon which they breathe! Question this doctrine and watch these money hungry pastors bare their fangs. This is a teaching that they will bear no compromise on tithing, or at least their own version of tithing, is their one true love.

Similarly, the *New Era* (2018), a government-owned newspaper, writes: 'At the moment a good number of the clergy are more preoccupied with material gains they derive from the tithing by unsuspecting worshippers who flock to the charismatic Pentecostal prosperity churches [...], for reasons other than grace and salvation.' Vitalio Angula criticizes the practice of tithing in prosperity churches, claiming it is characterised by manipulation and threats. He notes:

Great emphasis is placed on the followers to give 10% of their income to the church, along with other "offerings", contributions and gifts. These contributions are gained through several psychological tactics, with coercion being the main form of motivation. There is a subtle threat of God not blessing those who are unwilling to part with their money, and the corresponding reward of blessing those who do.

Namibian prosperity preachers are heavily influenced by Nigerian prosperity theology which 'shuns asceticism and seeks abundance in all areas of one's life' (Nogueira-Godsey 2016:256). In the mushrooming prosperity churches of Namibia (cf. Mulunga 2019) giving in general and tithing in particular play indeed an important role. Referring to passages like Malachi 3:10, prosperity preachers not only tell their congregations that they are stealing from God by not tithing, they also challenge them to test God by giving more to him. Basilius Kasera (2012:26), a systematic theologian and ethicist who teaches at the University of Namibia, speaks of the principle of a hundredfold return. This principle, central to the militant form of the prosperity gospel, suggests the more money people give to God, the more money they will receive in return. Kasera identifies several reasons why this message is so appealing to Namibians. He states: 'With growing social, spiritual, and economic issues which hamper living conditions PT [Prosperity Theology] claims to be holding permanent answers to these problems. It also presents itself as a way of hope for all the downtrodden of society and promises to offer a renewed spiritual vitality which the mainstream churches are said to be lacking' (:71). In 2018, the Namibian magazine *The Patriot* published an article entitled *Namibian Churches: A Story of Challenges and Hope*, in agreement with Kasera's observations:

> In the midst of abject poverty and increased violence, Namibians have turned to religion for relief. Subtle, effective and dangerously, religion and the worship of "men of God" has become widely spread acting as a substitute disguised as truth. But instead of spreading the message of love, churches are now infamous for [their] ability to lure followers into 'cult' type arrangements clouded with secrecy and fragmentation. Where churches once were an agent to unite people, religious activities are fast posing a threat to family cohesion and dividing communities. [...] Rituals to access God or blessings now include congregants compelled to eat sand and live dubious lifestyles, pastors who allegedly exploit the female flock sexually, desperate members seeking wealth and prosperity and the sick refusing medical care preferring holy waters coming all the way from Nigeria.

One cannot but agree with David Jones and Russell Woodbridge (2011:102) when they write that the doctrine of giving as it is promoted in prosperity churches is built on wrong motives. They explain: 'Whereas Jesus taught his disciples to "lend, expecting nothing in return" (Luke 6:35), prosperity theologians teach their disciples to give because they will get a great return.' In other words, while Jesus encourages his followers to care for others and to give selflessly, the prosperity gospel's doctrine of giving nurtures selfishness and greed.

Tithing and Good Stewardship

However, it is important to note that not every Namibian church that teaches and practices tithing falls into this category. Tithing can also be found in non-prosperity churches of a traditional Protestant or Pentecostal background, which consider it to be an expression of good Christian stewardship. Thus, Joseph Gawaseb (2020), a Namibian pastor, writes:

> Tithing is meant for individuals who understand who God is, [w]ho recognise that God is the creator incomparable, transcendent, immanent and owner of everything in this world and beyond. That is crucial. Without understanding these attributes of God, it would be impossible to understand tithing. I return tithe and give offering to the church, not to a pastor, because God told me so to do. He has also determined the reason to return a tithe, because I am his steward looking after his possessions.

Gawaseb continues to argue that tithing serves two further purposes: it encourages Christians to recognise their dependence on God and it reminds them of their covenantal relationship with him.

Conclusion

Finances are a hot topic for many churches in Namibia. How should churches raise money to support their activities and pay their pastors, evangelists, and other staff? Should mainline churches that rely on collections, membership fees, and fundraising campaigns embrace tithing? Or are there other principles of giving which Namibian Christians need to apply? What are the true biblical principles that should govern our giving in Church? All these are questions that require an answer.

To Tithe or Not to Tithe?
Biblical Principles of Giving for the Namibian Church

Johann van Wyk

Introduction

When I joined my current congregation as their new minister a few years ago I noticed that the congregation had no official policy regarding the issue of Christian giving. Shortly after my arrival, the congregational council decided to undertake a major building project, i.e. the building of a new church hall. Several appeals were made to the congregation to give towards this building project but, for a long time, the giving was below the council's expectations. Other Namibian churches that require members to tithe, i.e. to give one-tenth of their income, seem to be more successful in raising funds for buildings and other projects. My experience is shared by other church leaders. Victor Kuligin (2066:21), for example, writes:

> While working as a missionary in Namibia, southwestern Africa, I serve[d] as a pastor of a small church in the capital city of Windhoek. After several years meeting in a high school auditorium, we began to build a church on the outskirts of the city. For two years we raised enough money to complete the building up to the roof [...] We hoped that sitting in a church without a roof would spur our members to give enough to complete it quickly. Two Easters later, we still did not have a completed roof. Mercifully, God never allowed it to rain on a Sunday morning or during any other church meetings. A gift bequeathed to us by a faithful member who died provided us with enough funds to finance the roof shortly thereafter. It was over four years from the time we broke ground until the time we had a church building with a roof.

Kuligin continues by telling the story of a new prosperity church, which required members to bring a tithe each week (:21). The course of their building project was very different from that of his church:

During this time, another church purchased a plot of prime real estate in downtown Windhoek, on the main street running through the capital. In less than a year they constructed a church building five times the size of our church, a magnificent structure that could seat nearly 1,000 people. (:21)

This common phenomenon has encouraged me to look into the biblical teaching on tithing and to carry out a more in-depth study on the subject. The purpose of this research paper is twofold . First, it seeks to clarify the question if tithing is still an obligation for Christians and therefore should be encouraged in Namibian churches. Secondly, it seeks to identify principles of Christian giving which can help Namibian churches to deal with their finances in a godly way. Though my investigation focusses on Paul's teachings in 2 Corinthians 8:8-15, other Old Testament and New Testament passages are also examined.

Tithing in Scholarly and Popular Literature

Most authors, who argue that Christians have an obligation to tithe, place tithing within the context of Christian stewardship (Croteau 2010:59). Conrad Mbewe (2011:18), a Zambian Baptist theologian, for example, writes: 'If you are to be a good steward in this area, your financial giving in the church must be systematic and proportionate to your income. Tithing is giving to the church at least 10% of your income.' The notion that ten percent is the minimum a Christian should give is also promoted by John Bridges (1993:20) who writes about tithing:

> The old covenant 'written on tablets of stone' gave laws to be followed religiously, requiring legally-enforceable giving to the priesthood. We now live to serve Jesus as our priest, and the law is 'written on our hearts', so legal enforcement has ceased. But if God has given us a better covenant, should we give him less?

In his book *The Tithe* George Salstrand (1952:19) states that tithing was the historical practice of the Christian Church, while Herschel Hobbs (1954:17-18) claims that Jesus himself taught tithing. The same view is held by Keith Tondeur (1996:91) who writes: 'Jesus commends tithing in the New Testament in Matthew 23:23. Whilst He condemned the manner in which the Pharisees tithed, He indicated that this was what they should have been doing.' Larry Burkett (1991:36-39) stresses that tithing is not a legalistic practice but a demonstration that people are committed to God. Tithing is considered a helpful spiritual discipline that fosters spiritual growth. Michael Foss (2000:105) notes:

> [L]ike all spiritual disciplines, tithing often leads people beyond their original expectations. Many, if not most, of the people I have known who began to tithe, didn't stop there. They began with a commitment to grow to a full tithe, but once that goal was reached they continued to expand their giving. They did so not out of duty, but out of joy and a deep abiding trust in the goodness of God.

In his popular work, *Tithing: A Call to Serious, Biblical Giving*, R.T Kendall argues that withholding the tithe equates to robbing God (:20). The same point is made by Mbewe when he writes that '[t]the Bible considers lack of tithing as theft' (:18). For Kendall tithing has a strong spiritual dimension: 'Tithing, in any case, does more for us spiritually than it does at any material level. It releases the Spirit' (:27). The idea that there is a connection between the giving of the tithe and the receiving of blessings from God is also promoted by the American preacher and author John Piper. In a sermon on Luke 11:37-42, preached in 1991, Piper said the following: 'Finally, tithing will bring the blessing of God into your life in many ways. I see nothing in the New Testament that suggests that the promises of Malachi 3:10 are not valid still today for God's people.'

Some advocates of tithing stress the negative effects it has if one does not tithe. Stephen Olford (2000:28), for example, states: 'The principle of material giving to God is consistent and absolute throughout Scripture. When we give, God blesses; and conversely, when we withhold, God curses. So God says, "You are cursed with a curse, for you have robbed Me, even this whole nation."'

Other authors promote the concept of storehouse tithing. Storehouse tithing teaches that Christian believers should give their tithes exclusively to their local church. Lee Jenkins (2009:94) explains:

"Storehouse Tithing" means to bring your tithes to the church where your membership is established, your spiritual life is nourished, and your church privileges are enjoyed. If you give elsewhere, then it should be over and above the required tithe to your church, if at all possible.

A similar view is expressed by Mbewe and Tondeur who both stress that the local church needs the tithe in order to be able to carry out her mission. Mbewe states that the tithes together with free will offerings are '[t]he main source of funding for the church' (:17), while Tondeur writes:

Ideally, the local church should serve as the 'storehouse' today. After all, God intends the Church to carry out her certain functions which include looking after the poor and needy and reaching out to the lost at home and abroad. But even if your church is not doing all these things and you would like to support a Christian organization that is, remember you cannot sit under the teaching of a local church and not support it financially (1996:91).

While recognising that tithing is clearly taught in the Old Testament, Howard Dayton (1996:70) argues that the 'tithe is neither specifically rejected nor specifically recommended' in the New Testament. In other words, the Bible is unclear on how much Christians should give. Dayton holds that there is a reason for this lack of clarity:

I believe this lack of clarity is because the decision concerning the amount an individual gives should be based on a personal relationship with God. As we seek the guidance of the Spirit through an active prayer life, sharing suddenly becomes an exciting adventure (:70).

Other authors, such as David Croteau (2010), William Gregory (2003), James Quiggle (2009) and A. Bruce Wells (2011), are much stronger in their rejection of the idea that Christians are obliged to tithe. Gregory (2003:194), for example, writes: 'There is no scripture where Christ ever enjoined tithing on born again believers. Christ nowhere taught his disciples to observe tithing. Tithing was for the disciples of Moses, not for the disciple of Christ.' Wells (2011:viii), who shares this view, points out that one has to differentiate between tithing and giving. He notes: 'And just so there is no confusion, let me also say that when we speak of tithing, we are not talking about giving [...] The New Testament definitely teaches giving, but it never teaches tithing.' Likewise, Anastasios Kioulachoglou (2008) argues that, for Christians, the Old Testament law of tithing is as irrelevant as the requirement of sacrificing animals. He writes:

> The same reason that we use for not sacrificing animals is also true for tithing. Tithing was, along with animal sacrificing as well as other ordinances, part of the Mosaic law. Whatever is valid to one is also valid to the other. The Mosaic law became obsolete about 2000 years ago, with Christ's sacrifice. Together with it, animal sacrifices, tithing and the other ordinances of the law became obsolete too! We can learn from them, but they are not meant to be for our direct application. Is, therefore, tithing biblical? Yes it is. It is biblical as it is in the Bible. However, is tithing relevant and valid for the Christian? Here the answer is no! (:26-27).

The Concept of Tithing in the Old Testament

Tithing is a very prominent theme in the Old Testament. As John Goldingay (2009:652) points out tithing is seen as a norm throughout the books of the Old Testament and on into the New Testament. However, its significance varies. While the practice of tithing hardly changes, 'its aim and meaning are worked out anew in different contexts and connections' (:652). In this chapter, I will discuss some of the central Old Testament passages about tithing. I will show how the practice is motivated in the various contexts of the Old Testament.

Tithing in the Books of the Pentateuch

In the books of the Pentateuch, we read that people made different kinds of offerings. Offerings in the form of animals or food were given to God, leftovers were given to the priests or the poor (cf. Numbers 18:8-32; Deuteronomy 24:19-22; Exodus 23:11).

According to Joyce Baldwin (2009:119), the practice of tithing, i.e. the giving of a tenth portion 'to the God one worships is very ancient, going back before the law of Moses, and to other Near Eastern peoples'. That tithing was a common practice in the ancient world is also argued by Donald McKim (2001:1202) and J.A. Thompson (1974:180).

Pre-Mosaic Tithing: Genesis 14:18-20

Tithing in the Bible is first mentioned in Genesis 14:18-20 when Abram gave ten percent of the spoils of war to Melchizedek. John Walton (2001:419) explains the motivation behind this act when he writes:

> The meeting between Abram and Melchizedek takes place in the Valley of Shaveh. The designation of it as the King's Valley connects it to the valley just south of Jerusalem, most likely where the Kidron and Hinnom Valleys meet. The communal meal they share typically indicates a peaceful agreement. Hittite treaties refer to the provision of food in wartime by allies. Melchizedek is anxious to make peace with such a proven military force, and Abram submits to the chief king of the region by paying a tithe, thereby acknowledging Melchizedek's status by giving him a portion of the spoils.

Walton's interpretation is shared by Baldwin (1999:48) who writes that Abram recognized Melchizedek's 'superiority by giving him a tenth of all the spoils.' Derek Tidball (2005:326) explains Abram's action in a different way: 'It was a sign of Abram's gratitude to God for Lot's deliverance, voluntarily, perhaps even spontaneously, given, and it resulted in blessing for Abram.' Goldingay (2009:652), who agrees with Tidball's view about Abram's motive, reminds us that Genesis 14 does not mention any particular instruction about tithing which Abram received from God. In other words, tithing here 'is not a special revelation from God but a human instinct or a part of general revelation' (:652). Tithing is a human activity of gratitude towards God and Abram can expect Melchizedek to understand his gesture in such a way (:652).

Pre-Mosaic Tithing: Genesis 28:22

Another example of pre-Mosaic tithing can be found in Genesis, chapter 28. In 28:22 we are told that Jacob promised God a tenth of all God would give him: '[…] and this stone that I have set up as a pillar will be God's house, and of all that you give me I will give you a tenth.' Again, the initiative to give the tithe lies with the human protagonist and is not in response to a divine commandment or as Derek Kidner (1967:159) puts it: 'The gift of the tenth was voluntary before it was commanded.' However, this time the promise is made to God and not to another human being. There is no explanation in the text why Jacob decides to give a tenth rather than another percentage or how he would give the tithe to God (Davis 1987:87).

Walton (2001:572) points out that tithing was often seen as a means of taxation in the ancient world. Tithes were paid to the rulers or religious leaders. However, Jacob's tithe does not fall into this category. Walton writes: 'Jacob's tithe is clearly voluntary rather than imposed; thus, it is not to be associated with taxation of any sort' (:572). While Meisha Smith (2007:34) believes that 'Jacob's vow showed forth his thanks and faith that God would do what he said' Goldingay (2009:652) sees Jacob's promise in a more negative light. Referring to Jacob's 'calculating nature' he argues that Jacob saw the promise of the tithe as part of a kind of business deal. He writes:

> It is tempting to read his commitment cynically: "if you are going to look after me and give me food and clothing and bring me back here in prosperity and peace then you can be my God, and I will give you a tenth of all that you give me." Tithing can be a means of indulging in our instinct to calculate, a means of being selfish (:652).

Similarly, Croteau (2011: 61) argues that Jacob's promise could be understood as an attempt to bribe God. To support this view he points out that Jacob was an experienced negotiator and that he did not appear to be converted at this stage (:61). Croteau argues that the bribery of Esau recorded in Genesis 32 'demonstrates that Jacob still did not trust God's promises in Genesis 28' (:61).

However, whether we evaluate Jacob's attitude in making this promise positively or negatively, this passage demonstrates that Jacob thinks of tithing as a way of showing his gratefulness to God. He seems to think of tithing more as a voluntary act of showing gratitude to God than as a form of taxation.

Mosaic Tithing: God's Instructions

In the Mosaic Law, we can find four major passages that deal with the concept of tithing and which shed a light on the practice of tithing in ancient Israel.

Mosaic Tithing: Leviticus 27:30-33

During Moses' time, rules for the tithe were given to the Israelites (Appleby 1997:10). The Israelites were instructed by God to tithe not only 'grain from the soil' and 'fruit from the trees' (Leviticus 27:30), but also 'every tenth animal that passes under the shepherd's rod' (:33). Tidball (2005:323) explains the meaning of the phrase 'under the shepherd's rod': 'Strict enforcement of the procedure was enjoined so that the owner did not fix the results with a view to keeping the best for himself and giving the most feeble to the Lord.' Goldingay (2009:652) sees these first divine instructions as a warning to God's people not to try to evade the challenge of tithing. He writes: 'In Leviticus 27:30-33 tithing is simply an acknowledgment of God; you can't claim credit for tithing, and you must be aware of evading its demand' (2016:44). Croteau (2011:63) writes that one of the problems of Leviticus 27 is that it does not explicitly say to whom the tithes are to be given; it only says that they belong to God. However, Croteau has an explanation for this. He writes: 'This is because Leviticus is not directly compatible with Numbers 18 or Deuteronomy 14; it is simply an introduction to tithing in the Mosaic law.'

Mosaic Tithing: Numbers 18:21-32

While Leviticus 27:30-33 stresses that the tithe is for the LORD, Numbers 18:21-32 says that it was to be given to the Levites. Therefore, this type is also called the Levitical tithe (cf. Croteau 2011:63). In verses 21 to 24, the details of the Levitical tithe are explained. Verse 21 states: 'I give to the Levites all the tithes in Israel as their inheritance in return for the work they do while serving at the

16

Tent of Meeting'. In other words, the tithe is described here as a kind of compensation for their cultic service and is to be used for their livelihood. The same idea can be found in verse 31, which speaks of the tithe as 'your wages for your work'. Thomas King (2009) points out that the Levites 'worked as judges, administrators, cultic functionaries, and laborers'. Gordon Wenham (1981:143) comments:

> In recognition of their altar service, the priests are to receive parts of the sacrifice, first-fruits of the harvest and first-born animals. Most of these rights have already been mentioned elsewhere in the Pentateuch [...]They are reminded that members of the priests' families may eat from these offerings as long as they are 'clean'[...] These sacrificial dues compensate for the priests' lack of inheritance. Their inheritance is God himself, who provides for their needs through his people's gifts.

John Gibson (1983:143) points out that the provision for the priests is also called "covenant of salt" or "perpetual due". He continues: 'This is obviously an idiom for an irrevocable bond. Salt is invaluable in the Middle East, [...] Salt was a preservative against decay and so became a symbol for what will never decay [...]'(143-144). Instead of compensation, one could also speak of tithing as a means of ministry support (cf. Goldingay 2016:44). However, the tithe must also be seen as an inheritance as the Levites did not qualify for an inheritance in the land of the Israelites, i.e. they did not possess any agricultural lands which would provide them with a living. Croteau (2011:66) points out that the tithes were always from the agricultural increase. He continues: 'The Mosaic law never directed the Israelites to give of their increase; it specified particular products that were liable to tithes laws, and these products were always connected to the land. There was a very strong connection of products liable to tithes and the land.' As landless people, the Levites would not have been able to tithe as all the other tribes did. With the Levitical tithes, the Levites received an inheritance which enabled them to tithe. In verses 25 to 28, this variation of the Levitical tithe is mentioned. This tithe is also called the priestly tithe. Croteau (2011:63) speaks of the priestly tithe as a kind of 'sub-tithe' while William Horbury (2003:234) calls it the 'priestly tithe of the tithe' (2011:63). Croteau explains:

The Levites received the tithes from the Israelites and then gave tithes to the priests. There were basically two instructions for the priestly tithe. First, the amount was prescribed as one-tenth of all the Levites received as gifts. Second, the quality of the offering was to be the best of what they had received (:63).

In other words, the Levites were given an intermediary position between the priests and the Israelites, or as MacDonald (2015:104) puts it: 'They receive cultic dues, but are themselves subject to pay them.' It is from their inheritance that the Levites give ten percent back to the Lord as an offering.

Mosaic Tithing: Deuteronomy 12:17-19

The idea of the tithe as compensation or ministry support can also be found in Deuteronomy 12:17-19. Here the Israelites are asked to consume their tithe not in their town but in a place of God's choosing and not to neglect the Levites. Thompson (1974:171) speaks of 'sacred meals' which 'are to be eaten at the central sanctuary, and there alone'. These sacred meals are to be shared not only with all family members but also with any 'Levite who may be in town, in a spirit of happy rejoicing' (:171). Croteau (2011:64), who uses the term 'festive tithe', points out that the givers of the tithe are more or less identical with the recipients. It is not given to others. The festive tithe is kept by the people making the tithe. It provides the worshippers with all they needed during the time of the three compulsory festivals (see Quiggle 2009:16). The purpose of the festive tithe is to enable people to enjoy the Lord's presence and to rejoice in all their achievements with which the Lord has blessed them: 'There in the presence of the LORD your God, you and your families shall eat and shall rejoice in everything you have put your hand to, because the LORD your God has blessed you' (12:7).

Mosaic Tithing: Deuteronomy 14:22-29

In Deuteronomy 14:22-27 the festive tithe is more fully explained. Verse 23 specifies the place of sharing as 'the place he will choose as a dwelling for his Name.' In other words, the Israelites were required to bring the tithe into God's sanctuary. However, if that place was too distant the people were asked to exchange their tithe for silver and take the silver to the sanctuary (:25). They were to use the silver to buy food and drinks which they were to consume in a great feast (:26). Raymond Brown (1994:162) comments:

> When they came to the celebration meal, they were to eat it gratefully. It is all too easy to take life's blessings for granted. They were told that this was a reminder of how they had been *blessed by the Lord your God.* Here was an opportunity to acknowledge before others that he had helped them with their daily work. He had given them the soil in which the food would grow, the strength to till the ground, the sun, and the showers.

The purpose of the festive tithe is to strengthen the people's faith in the God of Israel. In verse 23 this purpose is described with the following words: '[…] so that you may learn to revere the LORD your God always.'

Finally, verses 28 and 29 describe the third kind of tithe: the charity or poor tithe (cf. Croteau 2011:64; Quiggle 2009:18). Every three years, this tithe was to be given to the Levites, the foreigners, the fatherless and the widows (Deuteronomy 14:28-29). By this demand, God made clear that he was 'deeply concerned about the welfare of all his people, rich and poor alike, and all the people must make God's concern their own' (Brown 1994:163). While in Numbers 18:21-32 tithes are clearly seen as support for a particular group only, i.e. the Levites, Deuteronomy 14:22-29 stresses that the tithes should benefit all people, including those in need.

Summary

When we look at the concept of tithing in the Pentateuch we can see that tithing is a rather diverse concept. In the pre-mosaic passages in Genesis tithing is portrayed as a mere human activity while in the key texts in Leviticus, Numbers and Deuteronomy tithing is clearly described as the human response to a divine command. The pre-mosaic passages describe specific situations that led to the giving of a tithe while the Mosaic law requires systematic tithing (see Croteau 2011:67.) The purpose of Mosaic tithing is (a) to acknowledge (to love and trust) God, (b) to express one's gratitude to God for his faithfulness, which can be seen in the way he has blessed the people's work, (c) to sustain the Levites, who have no land, (d) to support the ministry of the priests, (e) to enjoy fellowship with one another, and (f) to help all those in society who are in need. In other words, tithing serves the community of believers and their relationship with one another and with their God.

Tithing in Malachi 3

In Malachi 3 a promise of blessing is attached to the practice of tithing: 'Bring the whole tithe into the storehouse, that there may be food in my house. Test me in this', says the Lord Almighty, 'and see if I will not open the floodgates of heaven and pour out so much blessing that you will not have room enough for it.' The passage has been interpreted by many in such a way that tithing is a duty for Christians. Those who give to God what is due to him, i.e. ten percent of their income, and who do so through their local church will be blessed by God in return (e.g. Stephenson 2011:5ff). This kind of interpretation, however, is problematic. It overlooks the fact that Malachi 3 is first and foremost about God's relationship with his people. The main issue here, as Richard Taylor and E. Ray Clendenen (2004:429) note, 'is not tithing but apostasy'. The Israelites had turned their backs on their God. In verse 13 we read that they had 'said harsh things against' him. They had actually come to the conclusion that there was no benefit in worshipping the Lord and they did not hold back with that view: 'You have said: 'It is futile to serve God'' (3:14). As a result, all their religious practice had lost any sincerity or true value. While Taylor and Clendenen (2004:426) hold that their 'rituals of mournful repentance were purely exhibitions intended to attract God's attention and win his favour', Smith (2016:135) notes that '[w]orshipping God was [a] somber, joyless business, as boring to them as a funeral ritual.' The Israelites had put on a good show of empty religion.

In verse 8 God tells the Israelites that they rob him in tithes and offerings. Andreas Köstenberger and David Croteau (2006:69) argue that the phrase 'the whole tithe' in verse 10 suggests that they did not totally stop paying the tithes, but only paid a reduced amount. They write:

The prophet tells the sons of Jacob to bring the "whole" tithe into the storehouse. While this could refer to the idea that some people were tithing and others were not, it most likely means that the people were [not] giving but holding back the full amount required.

By doing so they were able to keep up appearances. The fact that they withheld their tithes in such a way was only symptomatic of their rebellious attitude towards God, or as Köstenberger and Croteau (2006:70) write: 'In Malachi, the withholding of tithes was a sign of a larger pattern of disobedience.' This larger pattern can be seen, for example, in verse 5. In this verse, God charges the Israelites with all kinds of sinful offences and announces that he will judge them: 'So I will come near to you for judgment. I will be quick to testify against sorcerers, adulterers and perjurers, against those who defraud labourers of their wages, who oppress the widows and the fatherless, and deprive aliens of justice.'

But then, in Malachi 3:7, God not only calls his sinful people to return to him but also gives them a promise: 'Return to me, and I will return to you.' This statement shows that God is the never-changing God who remains faithful and true to his people. He yearns for the restoration of their relationship, or as Croteau (2011:69) puts it: 'In spite of the people's sins, God loved them and patiently waited for them to return to Him.' God is reminding his people of his faithfulness and is calling them to repentance. This is the context in which the promise of verse 10 needs to be seen. If the people truly repent, it will be obvious. As a sign of true repentance and faith, they will stop robbing God and they will 'bring the whole tithe into the storehouse'. They will again acknowledge that their existence, even after the exile, is fully dependent on God. Baldwin (1972:245) notes:

> Israel has the opportunity to question His justice only because He is unchanging in His patient provision of opportunity for repentance. The prophet suggests a way by which the whole people can prove for themselves that this is so. The action he has in mind will so touch their pockets that their repentance will be costly and therefore genuine. The response of the Lord to this repentance will be immeasurable in material terms also when the next few harvests are reaped, and the man who puts

his possessions at God's disposal will find tangible evidence to prove that He accepts and blesses the giver.

Put differently, tithing is not a way to 'manipulate' God or a 'duty' which one fulfils in order to receive God's blessings in return. Tithing is an expression of gratefulness about the relationship that God has with his people. If they return to him, God will bless them.

Conclusion

While tithing had been instituted by God to provide for the priests and the poor and, as matter of fact, for the whole community, in the eyes of the Israelites it had become a useless obligation at the time of Malachi. With the increasing sinfulness in their midst, the people lost sight of the positive purposes of tithing; they lost sight of God's goodness which the concept originally reflected. They no longer saw it as a way of expressing their faith in God and their gratitude towards God for providing them with all they needed. They had forgotten that tithing was meant to strengthen them as a community and their fellowship with the God of Israel. Instead, tithing became a burden to them and they did their best to evade it. Their attitude towards tithing was a reflection of their spiritual state: They no longer gave their tithes because they no longer believed in a patient and loving God who waited for them to return to him.

The Concept of Tithing in the New Testament

The question that one needs to answer is whether the concept of tithing is still binding for Christian believers today. In the New Testament, we find four passages that explicitly speak about tithing. These passages are Matthew 23:23, Luke 11:42, Luke 18:9-14 and Hebrews 7:1-10. I will show that none of these passages have tithing as their primary subject and that nowhere in the New Testament are Christians commanded to tithe.

Matthew 23:23 & Luke 11:42

In Matthew 23:23 and its parallel passage, Luke11:42, we do not find any evidence that Jesus spoke against tithing in general or that he instructed his followers to start or stop tithing. Matthew records the following statement of Jesus, which is addressed to the Jewish religious leaders: 'Woe to you, teachers of the law and Pharisees, you hypocrites! You give a tenth of your spices—mint, dill, and cumin. But you have neglected the more important matters of the law—justice, mercy, and faithfulness. You should have practiced the latter, without neglecting the former.' The question of how far the law of tithing should be extended was debated among 1st century Jews (Carson 1995:480). It was a general consensus that spices were to be included. Jesus does not criticize the scribes and Pharisees for doing so. He accepts their practice as proper (France 1999:328). However, Jesus criticizes them for obeying the details of the Law but ignoring other directives of the Law in their general behaviour. Warren Wiersbe (2007:69) comments: 'They majored on minors. They had rules for every minute area of life, while at the same time they forgot about the important things.' Similarly, Douglas Hare (2009:269) writes that the Pharisees and scribes are chastised by Jesus 'for paying so much attention to such trivial matters as the tithing of garden herbs (which goes well beyond the explicit tithing requirements of Deut. 14:22-23) that they neglected the law's central demands: justice, mercy, and faith.' What Jesus criticizes is the hypocrisy which the Pharisees demonstrate. The hypocrisy of the Pharisees 'lay in their desire to appear conscientious about even the minute details of religious law' while paying no attention to issues which were much more important (Mounce 1995:217). It is clear from these words that Jesus considered tithing to be an aspect of the Law that is less important than doing justice or showing mercy, although we read in the last part of this verse that in Jesus' view the Pharisees and the scribes were supposed to tithe.

Some authors, such as Alexander Sign (2013:25), argue that the statement of Jesus in Matthew 23:23 and Luke 11:42, 'affirms, confirms, and establishes tithing as a biblical practice for New Testament believers.' To support this view Sign continues to argue 'that the law is a total package (James 2:10-11; Matthew 5:18-19) and that Jesus came to fulfill, not to abolish the law (Matthew 5:17)' (:26). However, there are good reasons why this passage cannot be taken as proof that Jesus expected his followers to tithe too. Firstly, Jesus does not address his disciples but the teachers of the law and the Pharisees who are still under the old covenant. Secondly, the main message of the wider passage, Matthew 23:23-36, is not about the practice of tithing but, as we have already seen, it is about hypocrisy. Jesus condemns any form of hypocrisy. He criticizes the religious leaders for outwardly appearing holy but inwardly lacking mercy and compassion. Michael Wilcock's comment is particularly helpful. He writes:

> Luke spells out the evil of their unrenewed hearts, but it is Matthew who records Jesus' direct and repeated accusation: they are 'hypocrites'. They are acting a part, which is what the word means. Their religious life is simply a role they play; it bears no relation to the kind of person they really are when off-stage. Their religion is no more than an outward show (1979:130).

One can only agree with Quiggle (2009:58) who concludes: 'The verses are hardly a call for New Testament believers to tithe. They concern the most legalistic sect of Judaism in an activity where they believed they excelled in righteousness over other Jews.' Thirdly, authors like Sign seem to overlook an important fact. As Ron Knott (2002:98) points out, the 'Pharisees tithed on the smallest of garden herbs and seeds, not because it was required of them, but because it was in keeping with the rabbinical ideas later codified in the Talmud.'

Luke 18:9-14

In Luke 18:9-14 Jesus tells the story of two men, a Pharisee and a tax collector, who prayed in the temple. The Pharisee said: 'God, I thank you that I am not like other men – robbers, evildoers, adulterers – or even like this tax collector. I fast twice a week and give a tenth of all I get.' What the Pharisee said about himself was strictly speaking true but he prayed in a spirit of pride (Morris 1994:280-290). He was convinced that tithing was among the works that would put him right with God. He 'congratulated himself that his moral life and good works made him righteous with God' while the tax collector was very much aware of his sinfulness and need for God's salvation (Quiggle 2009:59). The words of the Pharisee show that there was 'no sense of sin nor of need nor of humble dependence on God' (Morris 1994:290). He was, as Walter Liefeld (1984:1002) notes, futilely caught up in 'the fantasy of self-justification'. In other words, by telling this parable Jesus criticizes this very attitude, which leads to pride and which can easily cause people to despise their fellow believers.

David Jones and Russell Woodbridge (2017:131) point out that '[t]he reference to tithing in this passage is largely incidental'. The Pharisee boasted about his tithing, but he could have boasted about something else in order to stress his superiority. Therefore, Croteau and Köstenberger (2006:72) are right when they write that the main point of Jesus' parable 'is not tithing or stewardship but humility'. While Jesus does not forbid tithing in this story, he does not mention that the tax collector, 'who went home justified before God' (v.14), has actually practiced tithing. Croteau and Köstenberger conclude that this text does not provide an argument for Christian tithing. They note: 'It would be inappropriate and tenuous to attempt to draw any more conclusions concerning tithing from this parable. Jesus never tells people to stop tithing; he does say that tithing is part of the Law and that it should be practiced with proper attitude' (:72). The fact that this parable was not addressed to Jesus' disciples supports this view. Luke tells us in verse 9 that Jesus did not speak to his disciples but to 'some who were confident of their own righteousness and looked down on everybody else.' While Jesus expects those who tithe to do it with the right attitude, i.e. one of humility, this parable does not teach believers who belong to the New Covenant that they have to tithe. A. Cumming (2007:101-102) comments: 'Here there is no commendation of the Pharisee who paid tithes, and it was the tax-gatherer *"who went home acquitted"*. Again this verse cannot be used to suggest that Christ supported tithing for his followers; quite the contrary. Again, it is the Pharisee who referred to his tithing and, as already stated, a Pharisee is obliged to tithe.'

Hebrews 7:1-10

In Hebrews 7:1-10 the writer refers to a story from Genesis 14:18-20. It is the story of Melchizedek and Abraham. Although tithing is mentioned five times, i.e. in verses 2, 4, 6, 7, and 9, this passage is not about teaching Christians to tithe. As Kent Hughes (1993:187) points out, paying tithes to another person was a form of recognition of the other person's superiority and a visible sign of submission to that person. Abraham's payment of 'a tenth of the plunder' (v. 4) to Melchizedek needs to be seen in that light. Hughes comments: 'This was a calculated recognition by Abraham that he was in the presence of one greater than himself' (:188). In other words, the author of Hebrews clearly portrays Abraham as inferior to Melchizedek. The same is true of the Levitical priesthood. In verses 5 and 6 he writes:

> Now the law requires the descendants of Levi who become priests to collect a tenth from the people – that is, their brothers – even though their brothers are descended from Abraham. This man, however, did not trace his descent from Levi, yet he collected a tenth from Abraham and blessed him who had the promises.

The author stresses that the priests collected a tenth from the people not because of any superiority. No, the Levitical priesthood received the tithes solely because of one reason: it was a provision made by God's law. The tithe compensated them for their service. Consequently, one should not make the mistake to compare the Levitical priests to Melchizedek. They are anything but equals. While in the case of the Levite priests the recipients of the tithe are mortal beings ('men who die', v. 8), the recipient in the case of Melchizedek is still alive ('who is declared to be living' v. 8). The author continues to stress Melchizedek's superiority over the priests in verses 9 to 10. Donald Hagner (1990:103) comments:

> The point is clear. Since Levi was an eventual descendant of Abraham, he was in the body of [...] his ancestor [...] when Abraham was met by Melchizedek [...] and gave him the tithe. Therefore Levi may also be said to have tithed to Melchizedek through Abraham, and it is implied that Levi and his descendants are thus also subordinate to Melchizedek.

What then is the deeper meaning of Hebrews 7:1-10? What is the relevance of Melchizedek's superiority and unending priesthood? The phrase 'like the Son of God' in verse 3 indicates that all that is said about Melchizedek has some relevance to Jesus. Daniel Harrington (2005:47) writes that Hebrews 7:1-10 'concerns the excellence of Melchizedek, his person, his priesthood in relation to the person and priesthood of Christ.' The author of Hebrews presents Melchizedek as a type of Jesus (cf. Guthrie1983:157). He argues that Melchizedek is superior to Abraham and the Levites for three reasons. First, he received a tenth of everything for Abraham (vv.2&4). Secondly, he blessed Abraham (v.1). Thirdly, he is still "alive" while the Levites have died (v.8). David Alan (2010:411) points out that the writer 'establishes the superiority of Melchizedek to Abraham and prepares the way to argue for the superiority of the priestly order of Melchizedek [...] over against the Levitical order'. In Psalm 110:4 Melchizedek's priesthood is portrayed as type of Christ-like priesthood ('The LORD has sworn and will not change his mind: 'You are a priest forever, in the order of Melchizedek.''), which means that the purpose of this passage is to demonstrate to the readers of Jewish background that Jesus is in fact greater than the patriarch Abraham and his descendant Levi, i.e. that he is indeed the Christ. Hywel Jones (2011:72) summarizes the ultimate message of this passage well when he writes: 'If Abraham, the forefather of Israel and all the priests, humbled himself before Melchizedek, then so should the Hebrews before the one whom Melchizedek typified, Jesus, the Son of God. So should we – and the church of today – everywhere!'

Nonetheless, some authors refer to this passage in order to support their argument that Christians are obliged to tithe (e.g. Adams 2002:37-38; Brott 2008:31). Gregg Huestis (2011:123), for example, writes: 'The Book of Hebrews shows that the New Covenant Church was tithing in 65 AD, the approximate time in which Hebrews was written. In other words, the Church was tithing approximately 35 years after the ascension of Jesus Christ, proving that tithing was not some discontinued Jewish law.' Joel Parker (2003), however, demonstrates that this view is not without flaws. He writes:

> While it is true that the scripture says that Abram tithed to Melchizedek, it is clear that the account is about the one time described in Genesis 14. There is nowhere else an account to be found of Abram tithing to Melchizedek or anyone else for that matter. There is no reason to assume that he ever tithed again. This account cannot be used to prove in any way that tithing was a practice that Abram routinely did. To use the account in Hebrews as a proof text for tithing completely misses the

point that the author of Hebrews was trying to make, namely, that the priesthood of Jesus is superior to that of Levi [...] Surely, if God had intended for Christians to tithe, He had the perfect opportunity to emphasize that in this passage of Hebrews (:2).

The Law, the Holy Spirit and Principles of Giving

In 2 Corinthians, chapter 3, verse 3 Paul argues that Christians are the work of God's Holy Spirit. In verse 6 he continues to say: 'He has made us competent as ministers of a new covenant – not of the letter but of the Spirit; for the letter kills, but the Spirit gives life.' In his cmmenyary on this passage, Tom Wright (2014) states that there is a significant difference between the old and the new covenant: 'Jeremiah spoke of this in terms of God putting his law in people's hearts, and that is very close to what Paul envisages here. But the central thing he has to say, the central contrast between the old covenant and the new one, is now that God will give his own spirit to his people.' Keeping the Old Testament laws will not save anyone. It is God's Spirit who makes people spiritually alive. People do not become believers by following the law. God implants his Spirit into their hearts which enables them to live for him. Consequently, Christians should not put themselves under the laws of tithing. Russell Kelly (2007:137) comments:

God said, "I will put my laws into their minds, and write them in their hearts." The New Covenant laws of God are eternal moral laws which reflect his character. Eternal laws are clearly obvious in the mind and heart of every true believer. While the "giving" aspect of tithing may be eternal, the "ten percent" aspect is clearly cultic and not revealed by the Holy Spirit as a post-Calvary eternal principle. God's moral laws are not of the nature of tithing, which requires one person to persuade another person concerning that which is not obviously already "in the mind and heart." To restate the point, while giving may be moral, or natural, "ten percent" is clearly cultic and is not already evident in the mind [...] Paul and all other Christians are "ministers" of the "new testament". We are not called to teach or minister doctrines of the Old Covenant. Preaching the "letter" of the Old Covenant "kills" but preaching the "spirit" of the New Covenant "gives life".

Whenever Christians put themselves under doctrines of the Old Testament which are clearly cultic and not moral in nature, they are in danger of acting as if Jesus' death on the cross was in vain. They are also in danger of ignoring the freedom they have in Christ. In chapter 5 of his letter to the Galatians, Paul strongly rejects the claim that new believers need to be circumcised in order to become proper Christians: 'It is for freedom that Christ has set us free. Stand firm, then, and do not let yourselves be burdened again by a yoke of slavery.' To ask Christians to be circumcised or to tithe means putting a burden of law-keeping on them.

While the New Testament has a lot to say about giving, there are no explicit commands in the New Covenant instructing Christians to tithe. For example, in 1 Corinthians 9:14 Paul states that, 'the Lord has commanded that those who preach the gospel should receive their living from the gospel.' Put differently, churches have a responsibility to care for their spiritual leaders and to make sure that their financial needs are met. In Acts 20:35, Luke quotes the following words of Jesus: 'It is more blessed to give than to receive'

Conclusion

As we have seen, four New Testament passages in Luke, Acts, Corinthians and Hebrews all mention tithing. However, careful examination has shown that none of these passages are primarily about this practice. Their main purpose is to teach, respectively, the dangers of hypocrisy and self-righteousness and to demonstrate Christ's superiority. None of these passages positively suggest that there is an obligation for Christians to tithe. As we will see in the next chapter, the same is true for Paul's teaching on Christian giving which features prominently in chapters 8 and 9 of his Second Letter to the Corinthians.

Introduction to 2 Corinthians

Paul and the Church in Corinth

The relationship between the apostle Paul and the Christian church in Corinth was a very complex one (Kruse 2015:28). Paul visited Corinth three times. He also sent messengers to Corinth and received visitors from the Corinthian church while he was working in Ephesus (:28). Paul sent several letters to the Corinthian church and the Corinthian believers wrote at least one letter to him in return (:28). Colin Kruse notes:

> Due to the fragmentary nature of the information available to us, it is very difficult to reconstruct the details of the historical relationship between Paul and the Corinthians with certainty. Both our primary sources (extant letters of Paul) and the major secondary document (the Acts of the Apostles) provide only partial information. To add to the difficulty, our main sources (1 and 2 Corinthians) present us with some puzzling literary problems [...] (:28-29).

According to John Phillips (2002:9) the fact that 2 Corinthians is Paul's 'most personal and passionate' letter adds to the problem. Phillips continues: 'Moreover, he was dealing with a situation which was much clearer to him, and to his readers, than it is to us today' (:9). Furthermore, Paul was dealing not with one homogenous congregation but with several different groups of people in the Corinthian church (:9).

Paul's Authorship

Most commentators agree that 2 Corinthians was written by the apostle Paul (Guthrie 2015:5), 'though there are', as Gerald Bray (1997:xxxix) writes 'doubts about whether the current form of 2 Corinthians [...] is original to him.' Paul's authorship, however, is clearly claimed by the letter. The letter starts with the words 'Paul, an apostle of Christ Jesus by the will of God' (v.1) and in chapter 10, verse 1 the writer of the letter again identifies himself as Paul: 'By the meekness and gentleness of Christ, I appeal to you – I Paul [...]'. In addition, the letter is written in a style that is typical of Paul and it contains some serious rebukes which are also typical of the apostle when he addresses his spiritual children (Harris 2005:1). Finally, it contains some of Paul's most distinctive doctrines such as that of regeneration and of Christ's substitutionary sacrifice. Thus, Paul writes in chapter 1, verses 21 and 22: 'He anointed us, set his seal of ownership on us, and put his Spirit in our hearts as a deposit, guaranteeing what is to come', and in chapter 5, verse 21, the apostle declares: 'God made him who had no sin to be sin for us.'

Bray (1997:xxxix) points out that the letter cannot have been written before 49-51 AD when the apostle Paul was in the city of Corinth. He believes that it is most likely that the letter was written between 52 and 56 AD. C.K. Barrett (1973:4-5) dates it between the end of 53 AD and the early months of 54. 2 Corinthians was written to a church the apostle Paul had founded on his second missionary *journey* (cf. Acts 18:1-17). George Guthrie (2015:17) believes that Paul first arrived in Corinth early in the year 50 AD when the weather conditions made it easier for him to travel south from Macedonia to Greece. The apostle stayed with Aquila and Priscilla (Acts 18:2-3) and was later joined by Silas and Timothy (:5). Together with these co-workers, Paul founded the congregation through the preaching of 'the Son of God, Jesus Christ' (:1:18).

Form and Purpose

A number of New Testament scholars view 2 Corinthians, as Guthrie (2015:22) points out, not as one single letter but 'as a patchwork of more than one letter, pieced together by an editor once all the parts had been written.' The main reason given is that in several places the transitions seem to be rather abrupt (:22). Scholars who hold such a view divide the letter into several parts, varying from two to six (:22). Since they understand the letter as a composite of fragments, which were written at different times and for different purposes, they argue that there cannot be a single purpose or a unifying message (:35).

Other commentators, however, argue for the unity of 2 Corinthians. They stress that there is no textual evidence that the letter is a compilation of several shorter letters. For example, in his book, *Unity of Corinthian Correspondence*, David Hall (2003:87) asks some probing questions:

Why should a collage of Pauline fragments put together by a compiler be accepted without questions, by the Corinthians and by everyone else, as a genuine letter? If the compilation was made during the lifetime of the original recipients, they would surely have been aware of what was happening. And if the compilation was made after the death of the original recipients, one wonders how anyone could suddenly produce a supposedly genuine Pauline letter without arousing any suspicions.

According to Norman Geisler (2007:179), who treats 2 Corinthians as a unified whole, the letter can be divided into three sections. In the first section, comprising chapters 1 to 7, the apostle offers the consolation of God to those who minister, to their ministries and to all those who received their consolatory ministry. In the second section, comprising chapters 8 and 9, Paul discusses the issue of giving, whereas in the last section, which includes chapters 10 to 13, the apostle provides a vindication of himself to the group in the congregation which questioned his apostleship. Like Geisler, James Scott (2011) argues that 2 Corinthians consists of three parts. He writes:

> In the *first* section (chs. 1-7), Paul presents a defense of the legitimacy of his apostleship in the face of various accusations against him in Corinth [...] In the *second* section of the letter (chs. 8-9), Paul builds on the confidence that he has in the Corinthians by reviving his plan for the Jerusalem collection [...] in the *third* section of the letter (chs. 10-13), Paul prepares for his imminent third visit to Corinth by handling the problem of the opponents in a more frontal way than he has in the previous section of the letter (:4-5).

Other commentators have suggested a more detailed division. They hold that the letter consists of more than three parts. While Frank Matera (2003:25-26) suggests a division into four blocks, Jan Lambrecht (1999) writes: 'In 2 Corinthians five major parts, although unequal in size, can easily be distinguished: 1:12-2:13 (Paul's reliability); 2:14-7:4 (Paul's apostleship); 7:5-16 (Titus' return); chs. 8-9 (the collection); 10:1-13:10 (Paul's self-defense)' (:10).

With regard to the purpose of 2 Corinthians, Geisler (2007:177) distinguishes between one main or overall purpose and a number of sub-purposes. In his view, the overall purpose was to encourage the Corinthian Christians in their faith, while the sub-purposes were (1) to respond to false teachers who had infiltrated the church, (2) to defend his position as an apostle and his apostolic message, (3) to show both his trials and triumphs as an apostle, (4) to show the consolation which is provided in the Christian ministry and (5) to encourage the Corinthians to support the poor.

In contrast to Geisler, Scott Hafemann (2000:3) identifies a 'dual purpose' of 2 Corinthians. He sees the letter as a product of Paul's pastoral concern: a great number of Corinthians had accepted 'another view of Jesus, a contrary spirit, and hence a different gospel altogether' (:2). At the same time, Hafemann views Paul as an apologist who fights 'for the legitimacy of his own apostolic ministry' (:3). Murray Harris (2005:52) writes that the three main parts of the letter, i.e. chapters 1-7, 8-9, and 10-13 'have different although complementary specific purposes'. According to Harris, the purpose of chapters 8 and 9, for example, 'is to exhort the Corinthians to complete their promised collection for the saints at Jerusalem before his arrival on the next visit.' Together with the other purposes, this purpose serves one ultimate purpose: Paul is preparing the way for a third visit of the Corinthian congregation by removing any stumbling blocks that might prevent that visit from being beneficial to everyone (:52-53).

The Message of 2 Corinthians 8:8-15

My study of 2 Corinthians 8:8-15 shows that the apostle Paul touches on several important principles regarding Christian giving. Together with the surrounding passages in chapters 8 and 9, 8:8-15 forms, as Wesley Lindahl (2010:211) puts it, 'the most concentrated discourse on giving in the Bible.'

Introduction

According to Matera (2003:27), chapters 8 and 9 of 2 Corinthians were written by Paul to encourage the Christian believers in Corinth to bring the work of the collection for the church in Jerusalem to completion, or as James Dunn and John Rogerson (2003:1355) put it: 'Writing from Macedonia, on the journey promised in 1 Cor 16:5-6, Paul sends Titus and other delegates ahead to ensure that the collection (the main point of the visit) will be ready when he arrives.' Calvin

Roetzel (2007:42) stresses that, for Paul, the collection for the fellow believers in Jerusalem was 'an act of piety, love and solidarity'. David Garland (1999:364) writes that the collection provided the Corinthian Christians with the opportunity to practise generosity and 'to participate in something greater than themselves.' James Harrison (2003) believes that the collection serves an additional purpose. It would strengthen Paul's position as an apostle. He states: 'Thus, the collection represented a reciprocation of tangible material benefits that would secure his apostolic honour upon its completion, thereby creating a solidarity [...] and balanced reciprocity within the early Christian movement' (:311). Craig Keener (2005:202) argues that the collection gave the Corinthians the chance 'to demonstrate their newfound zeal for reconciliation' with Paul.

The obvious reason for the collection was a crisis in the Jerusalem mother church. The church in Jerusalem had been under pressure for some time and had, at least in parts, experienced economic problems. Charles Swindoll (2017:405) notes:

> The church in Jerusalem was in serious trouble, its very existence in doubt. By the time Paul wrote 2 Corinthians, the Jewish church in Jerusalem had already passed its twentieth birthday. During those two decades, the Jewish believers in Jesus had been increasingly ostracized, persecuted, arrested, tried, and shunned. Some were even boycotted, exiled, and executed. Their own countrymen, family members, and friends had turned against them.

While some commentators believe that the poor and famine-plagued members of the Jerusalem church were the exclusive recipients of the collection (e.g. Baker 1999:287; Roetzel 2007:41), others argue that the collection was taken for the whole congregation. Margaret Thrall (2004:509), for example, writes:

> [I]t seems that, according to Rom 15.26, the recipients of the collection are simply the economically poor members of that church. But this may be an over-simplification. First, according to Acts (2.44-45), the whole community was responsible for the economic needs of its members. And, secondly, it is likely that Paul had purposes, or a purpose, in view

in addition to the relief of poverty. Hence, it would be to the whole church, represented by its leaders, that the collection was to be delivered.

Roetzel (2007:41) mentions one of these additional purposes. For him the collection also had a strong symbolic meaning:

> While presumably, a significant number of the Jesus people in Jerusalem were impoverished, it was the combination of their need and the apocalyptic vision of the gathering of God's people that suffused the offering with symbolic power and offered a dramatic sign of the arrival of the new age when believing Gentiles would be welcomed into God's elect, and Jew and Gentile would be placed on an equal footing.

The same view is taken by Larry Kreitzer (2001:86) who sees the collection 'as a prime demonstration of the role that the Gentile nations play in bringing about the ultimate salvation of the nation Israel.'

Some commentators point out that there was a problem with the collection for the Jerusalem church which had been initiated at the Jerusalem Council. Ian Elmer (2009:173), for example, writes, that 'the collection was a point of contention between Paul and his opponents'. He continues to argue that it is possible that the collection had even been stopped as a result of this conflict between Paul and those who questioned him and his apostleship.

The Principles Voluntary and Cheerful Giving (Verse 8)

I am not commanding you, but I want to test the sincerity of your love by comparing it with the earnestness of others.

In verse 8 Paul is eager to tell the Corinthians that he is not giving them a command, though he could do so. As an apostle, he has that kind of authority but chooses not to use it. The Corinthians are, as Robert Hughes (1988:297) points out, 'free to do as they wish.' Instead, Paul tries to motivate them by comparing their love 'with the earnestness of others'; the 'others' being the Macedonian Christians. Linda Belleville (1996:216) comments: 'The Jerusalem relief fund becomes the Corinthians' opportunity to show, as the Macedonians have done, that the love they profess toward other believers is bona fide.' Simon Kistemaker (2007: 280) states that although Paul sees the need to use such a comparison, he excludes rivalry among the Christian believers by stressing genuine love as the basis. Kistemaker writes: 'His letter of love speaks eloquently of love that bans all envy, boasting, pride , and self-seeking (1 Corinthians 13:4-5)' (:280). Paul wants to give his blessing to the Corinthians as they show their love not to him but to their fellow believers in need in Jerusalem. He draws their attention away from their ego-centric focus to the outward needs of others (Swindoll 2017:409). Hans Dieter Betz (1985:60) argues that 'the object of the test was to prove the genuineness of their love, which would only be manifested by the successful completion of the collection'.

However, the successful completion of the collection should not only be seen as a test of the Corinthians' love for other Christians as Belleville, Betz and Kistemaker seem to suggest. It is must also be seen as a test of their love for Christ and for Paul who has been appointed an apostle of Christ (Vegge 2008:226). Thus, the words 'love' and 'earnestness' in verse 8 are exactly the same words that are used in verse 7 where they refer to the Corinthians' love and earnestness for the apostle (:228). Ivar Vegge concludes: 'Again, we see that the collection appeal and the appeal for reconciliation are concurrent' (:228). Hughes (1988:298) shares the opinion that it was Paul's intention that the Corinthians should give substantial evidence of their warm-heartedness as did the Macedonian churches. Similarly, Ralph Martin (1986:262) notes: 'Paul has no doubt about the genuine love [...] of the Macedonian churches shown in their zeal [...] for the collection. Now he wishes to be certain that the Corinthians share the same quality, both of love and zeal [...].' The amount that was contributed by the Macedonian believers is not mentioned by Paul, because it was not of importance to the apostle. However, what was of importance to him was the spirit of devotion and generosity. Paul knows that God does not look at the outward amount, but the heart's motive. This is a theme that we can also find in other parts of Scripture. In 1 Samuel, chapter 16, verse 7, for example, we read the following: 'But the Lord said to Samuel, "Do not look on his appearance or on the height of his stature, because I have rejected him. For the Lord sees not as man sees: man looks on the outward appearance, but the Lord looks on the heart."' Paul's words from 2 Corinthians, chapter 9, verse 7, seem to apply this truth: 'Each of you should give what you have decided in your heart to give, not reluctantly or under compulsion, for God loves a cheerful giver.' In other words, Christian giving is a very personal and joyful affair. One's attitude toward giving is clearly more important than the amount one gives. The value of a gift is not decided by 'its eternal magnitude but by the internal state of the giver's heart' (Hughes 1988:330). Consequently, every Christian must have the freedom to decide how much he or she should give (:330). Christian giving should never be compulsory but always voluntary, or as Miroslav Volf (2005:64-65) puts it:

> Since God gives freely, we should too. That's how the apostle Paul thought of gift giving; it should be voluntary. He praised believers from Macedonia for giving "voluntarily" to the poor in Jerusalem (2 Corinthians 8:3). Similarly, he urged that the Corinthians' gift be ready when he came to collect it "as a voluntary gift and not as an extortion" (2 Corinthians 9:5). Not only should Christian giving be voluntary but it should also be done in a cheerful manner.

The Principle of Gracious Giving (Verse 9)
For you know the grace of our Lord Jesus Christ, that though he was rich, yet for your sake he became poor, so that you through his poverty might become rich.

In verse 9 Paul mentions the primary reason for Christian giving, i.e. the self-giving of God's Son on behalf of humankind. It is because of his grace that Christ came into the world and died for the sins of the world. Paul uses this example because he knows that all believers are familiar with it. The sacrificial giving of the Christians in Macedonia is one thing, but the sacrifice which Jesus made on the cross for the entire human race is quite another thing (Garland 1999:376). In a way, one could say that the believers in Macedonia had made others rich by their poverty. Yet, they knew that they could never give more than that which Christ has given. No one had impoverished him or herself more than Jesus on the cross. Garland points out that this knowledge must have practical implications:

When we have been the beneficiaries of such undeserved grace, how can true Christians shut their hearts or purses to brothers and sisters in need or begrudge every penny they may share with others (see 1 John 3:16-20)? God's lavishness in the gift of grace and the depths of Christ's sacrifice requires that Christians be liberal in their giving to others. A half-hearted response ill befits the total sacrifice that Christ made for us (:376).

The connection between grace and giving can also be found in other verses of chapters 8 and 9. In chapter 8, verse 7, for example, Paul is asking the Corinthians to 'excel in this grace of giving'. What Paul is saying here is that, like faith and knowledge, giving can be gift of the Spirit, i.e. a charisma. We can find the same message in Paul's letter to the Christians in Rome. In chapter 12, verses 6 to 8 he lists different spiritual gifts that have been given to Christian believers. If someone has the gift of giving Paul urges them to 'give generously'. John Stott (2012:5) comments: '[A]ll Christians are called to be generous, but some are given the particular 'gift of giving'. Those entrusted with significant financial resources have a special responsibility to be good stewards of those resources.'

In chapter 9, verse 14, Paul again speaks about grace and giving. He writes: 'And in their prayers for you their hearts will go out to you, because of the surpassing grace God has given you.' Those who are gracious and give generously will be rewarded. They will be blessed by God and others. Their giving mediated through the apostle will create a bond of love and prayer between them and the recipients of their gift. Barnett (1999:155) helpfully comments: 'The receivers perceive that in the graciousness of the giver may be discerned the outworking of the grace of God in them [...] Both giver and receiver will know that God's grace, embodied in Christ, has started a chain reaction of generosity.'

Some authors have argued that Paul encourages the Corinthians to compete with their Macedonian brothers and sisters in their giving for the Jerusalem church. Jack Barentsen (2011:129), for example, argues that the apostle 'redirected the Corinthian drive for honour competition to compete for the honour in sacrificing for the benefit of other communities in their network', while B.J. Oropeza (2016:491) writes:

The Corinthians are prompted to consider in a fortiori fashion that if the poor Macedonians give generously and enthusiastically to the collection offering, how much more should they? Perhaps feelings of envy are also encouraged here, and an element of competition is employed typical of agnostic cultures.

Garland (1999) strongly rejects this idea. Commenting on verse 9, he notes: 'Christ's sacrifice becomes the real motive for giving, not trying to copy or outdo some sibling community. Paul asks them to respond to what Christ has done for them' (:378). One can only agree with Garland. Giving is an answer to God's grace in a believer's life. Verse 9 shows that it is modelled on Christ and not on the principle that competition is good for business, or as Rich Brott (2008:72) puts it, 'True givers are not motivated by competition; they are motivated by grace.' The best example of gracious giving is Jesus Christ himself. This point is clearly emphasised by the apostle Paul in this section. In verse 9 Paul speaks of 'the grace of our Lord' (*charin*), using the word 'grace' for the fifth time in this passage (8:1,'the grace' (*charin*); 8:4, 'the privilege' (*charas*); 8:6, 'this act of grace' (*charin*); 8:7, 'this grace of giving' (*chariti*)) (Swindoll 2017:409; Hughes 2006:192). Paul stresses that it is because of his grace that Christ 'became poor, so that you through his poverty might become rich'. Consequently, it is Christ's grace which should inspire the Corinthian Christians to demonstrate grace to their fellow believers in Jerusalem who are in need (cf. Garland 1999:379). Barnett (1999:144) explains what this means for the church today: '[I]n all matters related to giving and gifts we ought to imitate his generosity. Clearly, the self-giving death of Jesus is a major motive for our generosity.' Likewise, Kistemaker (2007:283) understands verse 9 as a call upon all Christ-followers, all over the world, to give abundantly to meet the needs of the impoverished.

Paul's statement that Christ became poor for our sake has been interpreted in a literal sense by some commentators. Lambrecht (1999:143), for example, writes that 'the term "poor" certainly does not exclude material poverty'. However, such an economic understanding of the phrase 'poor' is problematic. First, there is no evidence that Jesus was economically poor. As Garland (1999:377) points out Jesus 'was probably no worse off economically than any other Palestinian subjugated under Roman rule, and their puppets, client kings, and the priestly aristocracy'. Secondly, an economic interpretation of the phrase poor would imply that through his material poverty his followers were made materially rich (:377). This, however, did not apply to the Christians in Macedonia (:377). Consequently, the riches Paul is writing about need to be understood in a spiritual sense. According to Garland, the poverty of Christ 'must refer to something other than having no place to lay his head (Matt 8:20)'.

Barnett (1999:143) argues that the words 'he was rich' point to the pre-existence of Jesus and the words 'he became poor' to his incarnation. He holds that Paul gives an explanation of the phrases 'he was rich' and 'he became poor' in his letter to the Philippians. In Philippians 2:6 Paul writes that Jesus was 'in very nature God' and that he had 'equality with God'. Barnett points out that the phrase 'being rich' describes exactly the same, i.e. the fact Jesus was in every way what God was. He goes on to explain that the phrase 'he became poor' stands for the same as the words 'but made himself nothing, taking the very nature of a servant' which we can find in Philippians 2:7. It points to Jesus' earthly life. Jason DeRouchie (2017:19), who agrees with Barnett, puts it this way: '[B]ecause the poverty of Christ in 2 Corinthians 8:9 is focussed not on an abject material lack but on his incarnation (Phil 2:6-8), our "riches" point not directly to material prosperity but to salvation and all its benefits (1 Cor 1:4-8).' Paul's language here is, as Raymond Collins (2013) writes, clearly metaphorical. However, it is a language that is easy to understand for the Corinthian believers. As Jesus was willing to become poor for the sake of the Christians in Corinth, so they should be willing to share their material wealth with their fellow believers in Jerusalem and, by doing so, become a bit poorer.

The Principles of Desirable and Reliable Giving (Verse 10)
And here is my judgment about what is best for you in this matter. Last year you were the first not only to give but also to have the desire to do so.

According to Verlyn Verbrugge and Keith Krell (2015:172), Paul's focus in verse 10 is the Corinthians' desire to help. Apparently, the Christians in Corinth had the desire to collect money for the Jerusalem church and they were the first ones who actually donated money in the previous year. Paul now affirms their enthusiasm for the collection project (Dunn & Rogerson 2003:1365). Hafemann (2000) argues that the use of the word 'desire' here is an indication that, in Paul's eyes, the Corinthians have been truly converted to the Christian faith. He continues:

> As a result, to complete what they have started is advantageous for them as continuing evidence of God's grace in their lives. Not to complete the collection will signal that they are turning back on their earlier professed membership in the people of God. Understood in this way, Paul's argument is not one of simple expediency [...], but another expression of his conviction that genuine faith perseveres. The Corinthians' desire to give in the past cannot substitute for a lack of desire in the present. What began earlier, if it was genuine, must and will continue on as part of their restored faith.

Most commentators agree that the words of verse 10 must not be misunderstood. Paul is not pressurising the Corinthians. While Harris (2005:583) writes that verse 10 is 'an exhortation to finish, not a command to begin', P. Nicholas Kinnas (2013:5) states that Paul is 'merely keeping the Corinthians accountable to a Biblical principle that Jesus made and was repeated by James, his half-brother: Simply let your 'Yes' be 'Yes', and your 'No, No' (Matthew 5:37; James 5:12)'.

Thomas Stegman (2009) gives a possible explanation why the Corinthians stopped giving towards the collection. According to him, it is the conflict between Paul and members of the congregation which caused the latter not to participate in the project any further. Stegman writes:

> But the painful visit and its aftermath created much misunderstanding between Paul and the Corinthians. One of the consequences was that the Corinthians stopped gathering monies for the collection – a decision that may have been abetted by questions raised by the rival missionaries about Paul's motives and integrity (:207-208).

A similar explanation is given by Hughes (1988:303) who mentions a lack of trust in Paul as one of the possible reasons why the Corinthians stopped raising money for the church in Jerusalem: '[I]t would seem that their original zeal in this enterprise had flagged and indeed that, whether through natural apathy or through mistrust of Paul planted in their hearts by the false teachers in their midst, they had permitted the matter to lapse into inactivity.'

The Principle of Proportional Giving (Verses 11-12)

Now finish the work, so that your eager willingness to do it may be matched by your completion of it, according to your means. For if the willingness is there, the gift is acceptable according to what one has, not according to what he does not have.

While in verse 10 Paul is reminding the Corinthians that they once had the desire to participate in the collection for the Jerusalem church, he is now asking them in verses 11 and 12 to put that desire into action. Commenting on verses 10 to 12, Kioulachoglou (2008:34) writes:

> This passage deals with desires about giving and realization of these desires. The first part of the passage shows how important it is not only to give but also to desire it. It is desire plus realization of this desire that God wants from His people. None of these two alone works. God does not want you to desire to give but to never act upon it!

Verbrugge and Krell (2015:173) point out here in verse 11 Paul's word is straight forward: 'Now finish the work!' Paul reminds the Corinthians that they began with the collection a year ago and he now calls on them to bring their desire to fulfilment. Whatever it was that came between and stopped them from finishing the task must now be set aside.

It is noteworthy that, again, Paul does not mention a specific amount of money or percentage which he expects the Corinthians to contribute; let alone mentioning the tithe. Stegman (2009:199) concludes that, in God's eyes, a person's motivation is more important than the actual sum he or she gives. We can find the same idea in Luke's Gospel. In chapter 21, verses 1 to 4, Luke tells us that Jesus was more pleased with a poor widow who gave sacrificially, by putting two small copper coins into the temple treasury, than with the donations of the rich people. Thus, Jesus said: 'I tell you the truth, this poor widow has put in more than all the others.' The rich people want everyone to see how much they are giving, but the widow has a very different motivation: '[H]er heart is one that cannot hold anything back' (Card 2011:229).

While Paul does not expect the Corinthians to donate a particular sum or percentage, he formulates a principle of giving in these verses. In verse 11 he asks the Corinthian Christians to give according to their means and in verse 12 he stresses that they should not give according to what they *do not* have. In other words, their giving should be in proportion to their resources. Stegman (2009:199), therefore, speaks of the principle of proportionality. He explains:

> He [Paul] exhorts the community to give willingly out of what they have. Although Paul has praised the Macedonians for giving "beyond their means" (v.3), he clarifies that such extraordinary generosity is not normative. He probably also has an eye out here for the poorer members of the church in Corinth who might fear that their gift would be too small; thus he adds 'not according to what one does not have'.

As noted before, Paul does not mention tithing in these verses. However, he leaves the Corinthians with no doubt that the gift is 'to be proportional, not a percentage' (Rouse 2014:193). Paul's promotion of the principle of proportionality in these verses is a strong indication that he did not expect Christian believers to tithe. Harris (2005:587) writes: 'If Paul had advocated the practice of tithing, this would have been an appropriate place for him to mention or defend it. But so far from championing the practice of giving by percentage, he argues for proportional giving.'

The Principal of Fair Giving (Verse 13)

Our desire is not that others might be relieved while you are hard pressed, but that there might be equality.

In verse 13 Paul promotes the idea of equality. Some scholars speak of the principle of equality (e.g. Richards 2004:888; Welborn 2011:422; Wretlind 2006:81) or the principle of financial equality (e.g. Downs 2011:179) which is laid down by Paul in this and the following verse. Some commentators argue that Paul has a kind of 'economic egalitarianism' in mind (Little 2005:105). They suggest that Paul's teaching here is rooted in the Sinai covenant and that he calls upon the Christian church 'to conform itself to the Torah in sharing financial resources in order to achieve economic equality on a global scale' (:105). One could also argue that Paul is trying to impose on the Corinthian church the practice that was introduced in Acts 2: 44-45 and 4:32-34, which emphasises that the believers in Christ had everything in common.

The majority of scholars, however, disagree with such views. Barnett (1999:146) believes that Paul does not talk about equality in a material sense. The equality Paul is writing about is more of a spiritual nature. Barnett writes:

> He does not mean material equality as in an enforced per capita method of contributing which would reduce everyone to the same economic basis; it is a spiritual equality he has in mind. [...] According to the varying resources of each, there should be equal willingness to give so that one brother does not coast along at the expense of the too-great sacrifice of another. It is to be an equality of willingness.

Likewise, other scholars stress that the equality Paul is promoting must not be understood in absolute terms. The word *isotetos* which Paul is using here does not mean absolute economic parity (Bellville 1996:223). As Moyer Hubbard (2017) points out '[i]t frequently has the connotation of what is fair and equitable'. The same point is made by William Baker (1999:306) who writes that Paul seems to be more interested in equity than equality. While equality 'involves counting out equal shares of something', equity, Baker writes, 'is more concerned about what is fair' (:306). In other words, the apostle does not demand absolute economic equality for all Christian congregations (Sider 2015:92). He does not advocate a 'church wide community of possessions' (Johnson 2011:102), i.e. a communist understanding of equality (Welborn 2011:422). Paul 'is not insisting on equal distribution of wealth among all the churches in Macedonia, Greece, Asia Minor and Jerusalem' (Kunhiyop 2008:151). Thrall (2004:540) gives a good explanation as to why it was not Paul's intention to create such a general material or financial equality between the various Christian communities, when she writes: 'In that case, he would surely have been asking for assistance for the Macedonians, rather than accepting a donation from them.'

However, as Ronald Sider (2015:92) notes, '[t]he text at least demands an equality of outcome up to the point that those who cannot provide for their basic necessities receive generous supply from others.' When Paul talks about equality here it is sharing he has in mind (Cf. Coulibaly 2006:1433). In first-century Greek culture, a common aspect of friendship was the sharing of resources (Keener 1993:506). Through their faith in Christ, the Corinthians had become friends with other Christians. Consequently, their new-found faith 'required a more equitable distribution of provision within Christ's body' (:506). Put differently, Paul wants the believers in Corinth to take responsibility for their fellow believers in Jerusalem by supporting them financially. Hughes expresses this very well when he states that the equality proclaimed by the apostle Paul here 'is that of the effec-tive display of mutual respect and affection between fellow-creatures and fellow-sinners who by the grace of God have become fellow-believers in Jesus Christ and fellow-citizens of the kingdom of heaven' (quoted in Wretlind 2006:81).

At the same time, Paul argues for a healthy balance between giving and receiving in verse 13. He does not ask the Corinthians to give away all their pos-sessions so that they 'are left in dire straits' (Coulibaly 2006:1433). Neither does he want the Jerusalem congregation to prosper at the expense of the Corinthians. The fact that he uses the word 'relieved' shows this. Baker (1999:305) points out that the word 'relieved', as it is used here and in four other passages of the New Testament (i.e. Acts 24:23; 2 Cor 2:13; 2 Cor 7:5; 2 Thess 1:7), refers to rest or relaxation which comes after a difficult or stressful time. By using the word 'relieved' Paul underlines that the purpose of the collection is not about enabling people to have a luxurious lifestyle but helping them to overcome their economic hardship (:305). It is quite obvious that Paul wants to assure his readers that there will not be a situation in which the needy ones are enabled to live in luxury while those who gave are left in poverty. Garland (1999:382) comments:

> Paul is aware that some miserly members of the congregation might gripe, "Others will be profiting from our hard earned money." [...] Paul is realistic; [...] He therefore tries to deflect any possible complaint by assuring them that the Jerusalem church is not going to live the high life from these gifts. Paul does not ask the Corinthians to give more than others because they are better off. He asks them only to give what they can. The example of the Macedonians shows that Paul is not placing an unequal burden upon them. He does not want them to become hard pressed in offering relief to others.

Leander Keck (2005:365) points out that this concept of equality can also be found in Paul's letter to the Romans. In Verse 27 Paul writes: 'They were pleased to do it, and indeed they owe it to them. For if the Gentiles have shared in the Jews' spiritual blessings, they owe it to the Jews to share with them their material blessings.' Keck writes that this obligation to share is not a legal but a moral one (:365). By fulfilling this obligation believers express their 'gratitude for the benefits of the gospel, in keeping with the reciprocity ethos that marked the patron-client relationship in antiquity' (:365).

The Principle of Reciprocal Giving (Verse 14)

At the present time your plenty will supply what they need, so that in turn their plenty will supply what you need. The goal is equality.

Verse 14 further elaborates on what the previous verse says. Paul asks the Corinthian believers to take care of their fellow Christians in Jerusalem. Currently the former are economically better off than the latter. The Corinthians are blessed with material things and, therefore, have to take responsibility for their fellow believers who are going through a difficult time. Supporting them in that situation 'would be only fair, or equitable' (Baker 1999:307). By using the phrase 'At the present time' Paul emphasises that the support he is asking the Corinthians to give to the church in Jerusalem is not open-ended. The apostle is not expecting a long term, never-ending commitment. Similarly, he does not expect the Corinthian believers to give away so much that they would find themselves in a financially difficult position. Paul makes this clear by using the word 'plenty' (Baker 1999:307)

Furthermore, Paul assures the Corinthians of the reciprocity of Christian giving. 'Giving leads to mutual responsibility', writes Kingsley Rendell (1969:129). He continues: 'If they in Corinth gave according to their ability to the saints in Jerusalem then, at some future date, if there was need in Corinth the saints in Jerusalem could not possibly ignore them' (:129). Likewise, Keener (1993:506) argues that this principle of reciprocity corresponds to some form of modern health insurance: If the Corinthian Christians are ever in need, there will be other Christians who will support them. Keener continues: 'God always supplies enough to the whole body of Christ, but it is up to Christians to make sure that the "enough" is adequately distributed' (:506). The equality which the apostle has in mind is created by local churches supporting each other whenever there is a need (Baker 1996:308). This support, however, should not be limited to financial help. It can also involve spiritual or leadership resources (:308).

The message of verse 14 is clearly abhorrent to the popular idea and practice that churches are competing against each other. Verse 14 calls Christian churches to cooperate with each other and not to compete against one another. Miroslav Volf (2005:108) writes:

> Since God gives to all, and gives through each, cooperation can replace competition, and the gifts can circulate. As the apostle Paul put it, the present abundance of one party will satisfy the need of the other, and at some later point the abundance of that other party will help satisfy the need of the first one [...]

In verse 14 Paul encourages Christians to support each other and, although he makes it clear that he expects support in times of real need only, he is not promoting idleness. Thus, he uses the word 'need' twice: First, he talks about the present need of the Jerusalem church ('what they need'), and then about the potential future needs of the Corinthians ('what you need'). Paul is not asking to help fellow Christians who refuse to work. This is in line with his teaching in 2 Thessalonians, chapter 3, verse 10, where he writes: 'The one who is unwilling to work shall not eat.'

The Principle of God's Provision (Verse 15)

...as it is written: "The one who gathered much did not have too much, and the one who gathered little did not have too little".

In verses 13 and 14, the apostle Paul reflects on the principle of equality. In verse 15 he now applies a proof-text from the Old Testament (Joubert 2000:144). Paul quotes Exodus 16:18. Chapter 16, of which verse 18 is part, tells the story of how God provided the Israelites with manna in the desert. 'With this reference, the apostle directs attention to God, who amply fulfilled the needs of everyone during the forty-year desert journey of the Israelites' (Kistemaker 2007:289). By using this quote, Paul likens the Corinthians' money and possessions to the manna the Israelites received from God. The message is clear: their money and possessions are as much a divine gift as the manna was a divine gift. In the desert, when God provided the manna some of the Israelites gathered more than they needed and others gathered less (Exodus 16:17). However, everything was then put together and was distributed amongst the people. Craig Keener (1993:506) writes: 'Paul introduces the principle of God's provision by way of the manna in the wilderness; God meant everyone to have just what they needed, no more and no less.' The message that the Corinthians can trust in God's providence is repeated by Paul in chapter 9, verse 8. Paul assures them that 'God is able to bless you abundantly, so that in all things at all times, having all that you need, you will abound in every good work.'

God still continues to provide for those with needs by expecting those who have much to share, in loving kindness, with those who have less. T. Desmond Alexander (2016:94) comments: 'God's provision for food for the Israelites is a reminder of the need to be generous to others. We need to keep our desire for food, and other material possessions, in a healthy perspective. We should never be greedy for more, and we should never place these things before obedience.'

Lessons for the Namibian Church

The results of my examination of Paul's teachings on giving in 2 Corinthians 8:8-15 show that the apostle's teachings in this passage do not support the claim that Christians are obliged to tithe. Although Paul deals with the subject of giving at great length, not only in this passage but also in the surrounding passages, he does not mention tithing at all – neither explicitly nor implicitly. My investigation shows that the main motivation for Christian giving should not be an Old Testament commandment but God's grace. The giving which Paul describes in 2 Corinthians, chapters 8 and 9 is, as Croteau (2011:81) puts it, 'grace-driven giving'. Giving is an act of grace. It results from the grace of God which is at work in the life of Christians (Appleby1997:25). The apostle Paul leaves his readers and us with no doubt that '[g]iving is a matter of grace from beginning to end' (Hughes 2006:192).

On this basis, Paul formulates some very helpful guidelines or principles of giving. First, Christian giving is never by commandment. It is never compulsory but always voluntary. Second, Christian giving is proportional giving. Christians should give in proportion to their income/wealth. Third, Christian giving is a matter of the heart. Christians should not give grudgingly but cheerfully and generously. Forth, Christian giving is done with a willing mind. Christians give because they have the desire to use their resources to help fellow believers in need. Fifth, Christian giving is reliable. Christians should always strive to fulfil the financial commitments they have made. Sixth, Christian giving is fair giving. It helps the receiver but does not burden the giver. Seventh, Christian giving is never one-sided but reciprocal giving. Christians who give to those in need should get support from other believers when they are going through a time of hardship. Finally, Christians can have the confidence that God provides them with everything they really need.

What does that mean for the Namibian church? Instead of teaching the law of tithing as a divine commandment and, by doing so, burdening people in our churches, we need to focus more on Jesus Christ and his gospel of grace. If Namibian churches want to motivate their members to support the church and its various ministries financially it is important that they guide them into a loving relationship with Christ and help them to grow in their love for him. A strong relationship with Christ is the best foundation for giving. If someone's heart belongs to Christ, he or she will not question that everything else also belongs to him. If Namibian churches want to encourage their members to give generously we need to point them to the cross of Christ. As we reflect on the cross and what was achieved for us though Christ's death and resurrection, i.e. the forgiveness of sin, reconciliation with our heavenly Father and eternal life, we begin to understand how meagre our earthly wealth is in comparison and, as a result, our hearts are filled with thankfulness. In our churches giving needs to be a matter of the heart and not a matter of fear, force and threat; it also needs to be a matter of love and gratitude.

In our teaching, we should, therefore, not only elaborate on the above-mentioned principles but constantly remind our congregations of Christ's love and commitment for the world and his church, or as the evangelist John has put it in his gospel: 'For God so loved the world that he gave his one and only Son, that whoever believes in him shall not perish but have eternal life' (3:16). Jesus gave everything for us. Consequently, we should not hold back when it comes to the mission of the church and the support of those in need - both within and outside the church.

Namibian churches who do not promote tithing but have a system of fixed membership fees as their main source of funding need to rethink this policy too. It is certainly not helpful and an expression of Christian love when church members are refused services of the church, such as funerals or weddings, because of outstanding membership fees. However, this is not the only problem with this method of funding. While the apostle Paul stresses the voluntary character of Christian giving, membership fees are a compulsory levy, which discourages cheerful, generous and proportional giving. Namibian companies and parastatals may ask for fees for their services, however, Christian churches should not seek fees. Instead, they should promote a way of Christian giving which is in line with the teachings of the Bible and in particular of the New Testament.

In practical terms, this means that Namibian pastors and preachers should consider preaching a sermon series or offering seminars on giving. In addition to 2 Corinthians, chapters 8 and 9, they could base their teachings on passages, such as Matthew 5:42, Luke 3:10-11, Acts 2:44-45, or Galatians 6:1-10, to name only a few. However, they should always bear in mind what Richard Cunningham (2007:456) writes about giving in the New Testament, i.e. that '[m]ost passages on giving relate to God's gifts to us'. God has given us his Son, his Holy Spirit, a new birth, a spiritual family (i.e. his Church), forgiveness of sin, and eternal life. God is in the business of giving. Every good and perfect gift comes from him.

Bibliography

Adams, B. 2002. *Principles of Belief and Practices of Faith: A Guide to Successful Living, Part 1*. Coram: Bee and Gee Publishers.

Alan, D.L. 2010. *Hebrews*. Nashville: B&H Publishing House.

Alexander, T.D. 2016. *Exodus*. Grand Rapids: Baker Books.

Angula, V 2019. 'The Inner Workings of a Cult', *The Namibian* 7 May 2019. https://www.namibian.com.na/188231/archive-read/The-Inner-Working-of-Cult-VITALIO-ANGULAALPH; Date of access: 15 March 2020.

Appleby, D. 1997. *Explaining Christian Giving*. Tonbridge: Sovereign World.

Baker, W.R. 1999. *2 Corinthians*. Joplin: College Press.

Baldwin, J.G. 2009. *The Message of Genesis*. Leicester: IVP.

Baldwin, J.G. 1999. *The Message of Genesis 12-50*. Leicester: IVP.

Baldwin, J.G 1972, *Haggai, Zechariah, Malachi: An Introduction and Commentary*. Leicester: IVP.

Barentsen, J. 2011. *Emerging Leadership in the Pauline Mission: A Social Identity Perspective on Local Leadership Development in Corinth and Ephesus*. Eugene: Pickwick Publications.

Barnett, P. 1999. *The Message of 2 Corinthians*. Nottingham: IVP.

Barrett, C.K. 1973. *The Second Epistle to the Corinthians*. London: Adam & Charles Black.

Belleville, L.L. 1996. *2 Corinthians*. Downers Grove: IVP.

Betz, H.D. 1985. *2 Corinthians 8 and 9*. Philadelphia: Fortress Press.

Bollig, M. 2007. 'Inheritance and Maintenance among the Himba of the Kunene Region', in *Atlas of Cultural and Environmental Change in Arid Africa*. Kuper, R. (ed.). Köln: Heinrich-Barth-Institut.

Bray, G.L. 1997. 'Introduction to 1-2 Corinthians', in *1-2 Corinthians*. Bray, G.L. (ed). Downers Grove: IVP.

Bridges, J.M. 1993. *Mind Over Money*. London: Scripture Union.

Brott, R. 2008. *A Biblical Perspective on Tithing Faithfully: Going from Obedience to Blessing*. -: ABC Book Publishing.

Brown, R. 1994. *The Message of Deuteronomy*. Leicester: IVP.

Bruce, F. 1980. *1 and 2 Corinthians*. Grand Rapids: Eerdmans.

Burkett, L. 1998. *Giving and Tithing: Includes Serving and Stewardship*. Chicago: Moody Bible Institute.

Cameron, H. 2010.*Resourcing Mission: Practical Theology for Changing Churches*. Norwich: SCM Press.

Card, M. 2011. *Luke: The Gospel of Amazement*. Downers Grove: IVP.

Carson, D.A. 1995. *The Expositor's Bible Commentary with The New International Version: Matthew, Chapters 13 Through 28*. Grand Rapids; Zondervan.

Central Intelligence Service (CIA), 2020. 'Namibia', in World Fact Book. https://www.cia.gov/library/publications/the-world-factbook/geos/wa.html; Date of access: 10 March 2020.

Chiringa, K., 2018. 'Council of Church Shocked by Tax-Introduction', *The Villager* https://www.thevillager.com.na/articles/12740/council-of-churches-shocked-by-tax-introduction/; Date of Access: 18.04.2020.

Collins, R.F. 2013. *Second Corinthians*. Grand Rapids: Baker Academic.

Coulibaly, I. 2006, '2 Corinthians', in *Africa Bible Commentary*. Adeyemo, T. (gen ed). Grand Rapids: Zondervan.

Croteau, D.A. 2011. 'Post-tithing View', in *Perspectives on Tithing: 4 Views*, D.A. Croteau (ed). Nashville: B&H Academic.

Croteau, D.A. 2010. *You Mean I Don't Have to Tithe? A Deconstruction of Tithing and a Reconstruction of Post-tithe Giving*. Eugene: Pickwick Publications.

Cumming, A.P.C. 2007. *Balanced Doctrine: What the Bible Says*. Mustang: Tate Publishing.

Cunningham, R.B. 2007. 'The Purpose of Stewardship', in *Leadership Handbook of Management and Administration*. Berkley, J.D. (ed). Grand Rapids: Baker Books

Davis, G.B. 1987. Are Christians Supposed to Tithe?. *Criswell Theological Review* 2(1):85-97.

Dayton, H 1996. *Your Money Counts: (How More Than Ever)*. Carol Stream: Tyndale House.

DeRouchie, J.S. 2017. Is *Every* Promise "Yes"? Old Testament Promises and the
Christian. *Themelios* 42(1):16-45.

Downs, D.J. 2011. '2 Corinthians', in *Dictionary of Scripture and Ethics*. Green, J.B.
(ed). Grand Rapids: Baker Academic.

Dunn, J.D. G. 2006. *Christian Liberty: A New Testament Perspective*. Nottingham:
Alpha Graphics.

Dunn, D.G & Rogerson, J.W. 2003. *Eerdmans Commentary on the Bible*. Grand
Rapids: Eerdmans.

Ejikeme, A 2011. *Culture and Customs of Namibia*. Santa Barbara: Greenwood.

Elmer, I.J. 2009. *Paul, Jerusalem and the Judaisers: The Galatian Crisis in its
Broadest Historical Context*. Tübingen: Mohr Siebeck.

Evangelical Lutheran Church in the Republic of Namibia, 2009. *Constitution of the
Evangelical Lutheran Church in The Republic of Namibia*.

Foss, M.W. *Power Surge: Six Marks of Discipleship for a Changing Church*.
Minneapolis: Fortress Press.

France, R.T. 1985. *The Gospel According to Matthew: An Introduction and
Commentary*. Leicester: IVP.

Garland, D.E. 1999. *2 Corinthians*. Nashville: B&H Publishing.

Gawseb, J 2014. 'Tithing is Covenant with God', letter to *The Namibian*,
published 23 May 2014.
https://www.namibian.com.na/index.php?id=123582&page=archive-read Date
of access: 16 March 2020.

Geisler, N.L. 2007. *A Popular Survey of the New Testament*. Grand Rapids. Baker
Books.

Gibson, J.C.L. 1983. *Number*s. Edinburgh: The Saint Andrew Press.

Goetz, R. 1997. Gratitude for Everything. *Christian Century* 114(22):689.

Goldingay, J. 2016. *An Introduction to the New Testament: Exploring Texts,
Approaches and Issues*. London: SPCK.

Goldingay, J. 2009. *The Old Testament Theology, Volume Three: Israel's Life*.
Downers Grove: IVP.

Gregory, W.T. 2003. *What Tithing Is Not, What Nation Is He Speaking To?* -: Xulon Press.

Guthrie, D. 1983. *Hebrews*. Leicester: IVP.

Guthrie, G.H. 2015. *2 Corinthians*. Grand Rapids: Baker Academic.

Hafemann, S.J. 2000. *The NIV Application Commentary: 2 Corinthians*. Grand Rapids: Zondervan.

Hagner, D.A. 1995. *Hebrews*. Peabody; Hendrickson Publishers.

Hall, D.R. 2003. *The Unity of the Corinthian Correspondence*. London: T & T Clark International.

Hare, D.R.A. 2009. *Matthew*. Louisville: Westminster John Knox Press.

Harrington, D.J. 2005. *What Are They Saying About the Letter to the Hebrews?* New York: Paulist Press.

Harris, M.J. 2005. *The Second Epistle to the Corinthians: A Commentary on the Greek Text*. Grand Rapids: Eerdmans.

Harrison, J.R. 2003. *Paul's Language of Grace in Its Graeco-Roman Context*. Eugene: Wipf & Stock.

Hobbs, H.H. 1954. *The Gospel of Giving*. Nashville: Broadman Press.

Hooker, M.D. 2008. *Paul: A Beginner's Guide*. Oxford: Oneworld Publications.

Horbury, W. 2003. *Messianism Among Jews and Christians: Twelve Biblical and Historical Studies*. London: T & T Clark.

Hubbard, M.V. 2017. *Second Corinthians*. Grand Rapids: Baker Books.

Huestis, G.N. 2011. *When the Holy Spirit Reveals: New Insights into Old Controversies*. Ft. Collins: Blessed To Be A Blessing Ministry.

Hughes, P.E. 1988. *Paul's Second Epistle to the Corinthians*. Grand Rapids: Eerdmans.

Hughes, R.K. 2006. Disciplines of a Godly Man. Wheaton: Crossway.

Hughes, R.K.1993. *Hebrews: An Anchor for the Soul*. Wheaton: Crossway Books.

Jenkins, L. 2009. *Lee Jenkins on Money: Real Solutions to Financial Challenges*. Chicago: Moody Publishers.

Johnson, L.T. 2011. *Sharing Possessions: What Faith Demands*. Grand Rapids: Eerdmans.

Jones, D.W. & Woodbridge, R.S. 2017. *Health, Wealth and Happiness: How the Prosperity Gospel Overshadows the Gospel of Christ*. Grand Rapids: Kregel.

Jones, H.R. 2011. *Let's Study Hebrews*. Edinburgh: The Banner of Truth Trust.

Joubert, S. 2000. *Paul as Benefactor: Reciprocity, Strategy and Theological Reflection in Paul's Collection*. Eugene: Wipf & Stock.

Kambowe, K. 2019. 'Commercial Tax Coming for Churches, NGOs', *Namibian Sun* 21.10.2019. https://www.namibiansun.com/news/commercial-tax-coming-for-churches-ngos-2019-10-21; Date of Access: 18.04.2020.

Keck, L.E. 2005. *Romans*. Nashville: Abingdon Press.

Keener, C.S. 2005. *1-2 Corinthians*. Cambridge: Cambridge University Press.

Keener, C.S. 1993. *The IVP Background Commentary: New Testament*. Downers Grove: IVP.

Kelly, R.E. 2007. *Should the Church Teach Tithing? A Theologian's Conclusions About A Taboo Doctrine*. Lincoln: iUniverse.

Kendall, R.T. 1982. *Tithing: A Call to Serious, Biblical Giving*. London: Hodder & Stoughton.

Kidner, D 1967. *Genesis*. Leicester: IVP.

King, T.J. 2009. *The Realignment of the Priestly Literature: The Priestly Narrative in Genesis and its Relation to Priestly Legislation and the Holiness School*. Eugene: Pickwick Publications.

Kinnas, P.N. 2013. *Difficult Bible Topics: A Close Look At Challenging and Misunderstood Issues Christians Face*. Bloomington: WestBow Press.

Kioulachoglou, A. 2008. *Tithing, Giving and the New Testament: bringing Centuries-long Practices and Traditions to the Light of Scripture*. -: Xulon Press.

Kistemaker, S.J. 2007. *New Testament Commentary: Exposition of the Second Epistle to the Corinthians*. Grand Rapids: Baker Academic.

Knott, R. 2002. *God's Guarantees for Giving: A Biblical Look at the Law of Tithing...Was it Rescinded by Grace?* Fairfax: Xulon Press.

Köstenberger, A.J. & Croteau D.A. 2006. "Will A Man Rob God?" (Malachi 3:8): A Study of Tithing in the Old and New Testaments. *Bulletin for Biblical Research* 16(1):53-77.

Kreitzer, L. 2001. *2 Corinthians*. Sheffield: Sheffield Academic Press.

Kruse, C.G. 2015. *2 Corinthians,* Revised Edition. Downers Grove: IVP.

Kuligin, V 2006. *Ten Things I Wish Jesus Never Said*. Wheaton: Crossway Bookds.

Kunhiyop, S.W. 2008. *Africa Christian Ethics*. Nairobi: Hippo Books.

Lamb, J. 1990. *2 Corinthians*. Leicester: Crossway Books.

Lambrecht, J. 1999.*Second Corinthians*. Collegeville: The Liturgical Press.

Lebert, J. 2005. 'Inheritance Practices and Property Rights in Ohangwena Region', in
The Meaning of Inheritance: Perspectives on Namibian Inheritance Practices.
Windhoek: Legal Assistance Centre.

Liefeld, W.L. 1986. 'Luke', in *The Expositor's Bible Commentary, Volume 8,*
Gaebelein, F.E (gen. ed.). Grand Rapids: Zondervan.

Lim, K.Y. 2013. Generosity from Pauline Perspective: Insights from Paul's Letters to
the Corinthians. *Evangelical Review of Theology* 37(1):20-33.

Lindahl, W.E. 2010. *Principles of Fundraising: Theory and Practice*. Boston: Jones
and Bartlett Publishers.

Little, C.R. 2005. *Mission in the Way of Paul: Biblical Mission for the Twenty-first
Century*. New York: Peter Lang.

Lutheran Communion on Southern Africa, *Strategy 2013-2017: A Work in Progress*,
11. http://www.elcz.co.zw/uploads/1/1/4/0/11402736/lucsa_2013-
2017_strategic_plan.pdf; Date of access: 18.04.2020.

MacDonald, N. 2015. *Priestly Rule: Polemical and Biblical Interpretation in Ezekiel
44*. Berlin: De Gruyter.

Martin, R.P. 1986. *2 Corinthians*. Waco: Word Books.

Matera, F.J. 2003.*II Corinthians: A Commentary*. Louisville: Westminster John Knox
Press.

Mbewe, C. 2011. *Foundations of the Flock: Truths About the Church for All the
Saints*. Hannibal: Granted Ministries Press.

McComiskey, T.E. 1998. *The Minor Prophet: An Exegetical and Expository
Commentary, Vol 3*. Grand Rapids: Michigan.

McKim, D. 2001.'Tithing', in *Evangelical Dictionary of Theology*, Elwell, W.A. (ed).
Grand Rapids: Baker Academic.

Melber, H. 2020. 'Namibia is Showing Wear and Tear after 30 Years under SWAPO Rule.' *The Conversation* 17 March 2020. theconversation.com/namibia-is-showing-wear-and-tear-after-30-years-under-swapo-rule-133703; Date of access: 20 March 2020.

Morris, L. 1995. *The Gospel According to Matthew*. Leicester: IVP.

Morris, L. 1994. *Luke: An Introduction and Commentary*. Leicester: IVP.

Mounce, R.H. 1998. *Matthew*. Peabody: Hendrickson Publishers.

Mulunga, E. 2019. 'Regulate Churches in Namibia'. *The Namibian* 4 October 2019. https://www.namibian.co.na/193842/archive-read/Regulate-Churches-in-Namibia-EMILIA-MULUNGAMAJOR; Date of access: 19 March 2020.

Murray, S. 2011. *Beyond Tithing*. Eugene: Wipf & Stock.

Mwinga, M.S 2012. *The Role of Churches in Namibia's Economic Development*. Windhoek: First Capital Research.

Nangula, E.M. 2013. *The Role of the Evangelical Lutheran Church in Namibia (ELCN) as a Pioneer of Social Development Through Education in Ovamboland (1870-1970): A Church Historical Study*. Unpublished MTh dissertation, University of Stellenbosch.

Nogueira-Godsey, T. 2016. 'Rising to the Challenge: Pentecostalism in Angola, Botswana, and Namibia', *in Global Renewal Ministry: Spirit-Empowered Movements: Past, Present, and Future, Volume 3: Africa*, V. Synan, A. Young, J.K. Asamoah- Gyadu (eds.). Lake Mary: Charisma House.

Olford, S.F. 2000. *The Grace of Giving: A Biblical Study of Christian Stewardship*. Grand Rapids: Kregel.

O'Mahony, K. 2000. *Pauline Persuasion: A Sounding in 2 Corinthians 8-9*. Sheffield: Sheffield Academic Press.

O'Neill, S. 1999. 'A Shoestring and a Prayer', *Kiplinger's Personal Finance Magazine* May.

Oropeza, B.J. 2016. *Exploring Second Corinthians: Death and Life, Hardship and Rivalry*. Atlanta: SBL Press.

Parker, J. 2003. *Tithing in the Age of Grace*. Victoria: Trafford Publishing.

Phillips, J. 2002. *Exploring 2 Corinthians: An Expository Commentary*. Grand Rapids: Kregel Publications.

Piper, J. 1991. 'These You Ought to Have Done Without Neglecting the Other', sermon preached on 13th January 1991. http"//www.desiringod.org/messages/these-you-ought-to-have-done-without-neglecting-the-others; Date of access: 6 March 2017.

Powell, M.A. 2006. *Giving to God: The Bible's Good News about Living a Generous Life*. Grand Rapids: Eerdmans.

Prime, D. 2000. *Let's Study 2 Corinthians*. Edinburgh: Banner of Truth.

Pusey, E.B. 1950. *The Minor Prophets, A Commentary, Vol 2*. Grand Rapids 6, Michigan.

Quiggle, J.D. 2009. *Why Christians Should Not Tithe: A History of Tithing and a Biblical Paradigm for Christian Giving*. Eugene: Wipf & Stock.

Rendell, K.G 1969. *Expository Outlines from 1 and 2 Corinthians*. London: Pickering & Inglis.

Richards, L.O. 2004. *Bible Teacher's Commentary*. Eastbourne: Victor.

Roetzel, C.J. 2007. *2 Corinthians*. Nashville: Abingdon Press.

Rouse, J.D. 2014. *Paul, the Passionate Scholar*. Bloomington: WestBow Press.

Salstrand, G.A.E. 1952, *The Tithe: The Minimum Standard for Christian Giving*. Grand Rapids: Baker Books.

Scott, J.M. 2011. *2 Corinthians*. Grand Rapids: Baker Books.

Shivute, O. 2012. 'ELCIN is N$2 million in the red', *The Namibian* 25 April 2012. http://www.namibian.com.na/94445/archive-read/ELCIN-is-N$2-million-in-the-red-THE-Evangelical; Date of access: 13 March 2020.

Sider, R. 2015. *Rich Christians in an Age of Hunger: Moving from Affluence to Generosity*. -: W Publishing Group.

Sign, A.O. 2013. *Tithe: Obsolete or Relevant?* Bloomington: AuthorHouse.

Smith J.E. 2016. *Haggai & Malachi: A Christian Interpretation*.

Smith, K.G. undated. *How to Do an Exegetical Study*. South African Theological Seminary. http://www.sats.edu.za/userfiles/Smith,Howtodoanexegeticalstudy.pdf; Date of access: 25 February 2017.

Smith, M.L. 2007. *The Joy and Truth of Tithing*. -: Xulon Press.

Stegman, T. 2009. *Second Corinthians*. Grand Rapids: Baker Academic.

Stenschke, C. 2012. The Current Financial Crisis of Europe: Paul's Collection for Jerusalem and Good Stewardship. *European Journal of Theology* 21(2):97-99.

Stephenson, P.R. 2011. *Tithing and How to Get There: The Short Course*. Raleigh: Lulu Enterprises.

Stott, J. 2012. *The Grace of Giving: Ten Principles of Christian Giving*. London: Langham Partnership International & International Fellowship of Evangelical Students.

Swindoll, C.R. 2017. *Insights on 1 & 2 Corinthians*. Carol Stream: Tyndale House Publishers.

Taylor, R.A. & Clendenen, E.R. 2004, *Haggai, Malachi, Vol. 21A, The New American Commentary*. Nashville: Broadman & Holman Publishers.

Thompson, J.A. 1974. *Deuteronomy*. Leicester: IVP.

Thrall, M.E. 2004. *A Critical Commentary on the Second Epistle to the Corinthians, Volume II*. London; T&T Clark.

Tidball, D. 2005. *The Message of Leviticus*. Leicester: IVP.

Tjimbundu, M 2018. 'Of Katutura Churches in White Gowns', *The Villager* https://www.thevillager.com.na/articles/735/of-katutura-churches-in-white-gowns/; Date of access: 21 March 2020.

Tonchi, V.L, Lindeke, W.A. & Grotpeter, J.J. 2012. *Historical Dictionary of Namibia*. Lanham: The Scarecrow Press.

Tondeur, K. 1996. *Your Money and Your Life: Learning How to Handle Money God's Way*. London: Triangle SPCK.

Vegge, I. 2008. *2 Corinthians – A Letter About Reconciliation: A Psychological, Epistolographical and Rhetorical Analysis*. Tübingen: Mohr Siebeck.

Verbrugge, V. & Krell, K.R. 2015. *Paul and Money: A Biblical and Theological Analysis of the Apostle's Teachings and Practices.* Grand Rapids: Zondervan.

Volf, M. 2005. *Free of Charge: Giving and Forgiving in a Culture Stripped of Grace.* Grand Rapids: Zondervan.

Walton, J.H. 2001. *Genesis: the NIV Application Commentary.* Grand Rapids: Zondervan.

Welborn, L.L. 2011. *An End to Enmity: Paul and the "Wrongdoer" of Second Corinthians.* Berlin: Walter de Gruyter.

Wells, A.B. 2011. *Tithing: Nailed to the Cross.* Bloomington: AuthorHouse.

Wenham, G.J. 1981. *Numbers: An Introduction & Commentary.* Leicester: IVP.

Wiersbe, W.W. 2007. *The Wiersbe Bible Commentary: New Testament.* Colorado Springs: David C. Cook.

Wilcock, M 1979. *The Message of Luke: The Saviour of the World.* Leicester: IVP.

World Bank 2019. 'The World Bank in Namibia: Overview'. https://www.worldbank.org/en/country/namibia/overview; Date of access: 10 March 2020.

World Council of Churches 2020. 'Evangelical Lutheran Church in the Republic of Namibia', https://www.oikoumene.org/en/member-churches/evangelical-lutheran-church-in-the-republic-of-namibia; Date of Access: 18.04.2020.

Wretlind, D.O. 2006. *Shekels, Dollars, and Sense.* Victoria: Trafford Publishing.

Wright, T. 2014. *Paul for Everyone: Second Corinthians.* London: SPCK.

'Namibian Churches: A Story of Challenges and Hope', *The Patriot*, 24 August 2018, https://thepatriot.com.na/index.php/2018/08/24/namibian-churches-a-story-of-challenges-and-hope/; Date of access: 4 March 2020.

'The Role of Faith Not So Well In Namibia (Part 2)', *New Era* 12 May 2017 https://neweralive.na/posts/the-role-of-faith-in-not-so-well-namibia-part-2; Date of access: 21 March 2020.

'!Gawaxab Donates Half-a-million to Church', *The Namibian* 4 September 2018. https://www.namibian.com.na/181063/archive-read/Gawaxab-donates-half-a-million-to-church; Date of access: 23 March 2020.

About the Authors

Johann van Wyk *BTh (Hon), DipTh*

Johann van Wyk is the minister of the Windhoek congregation of the Rhenish Church in Namibia. Formerly, he served in congregations of his church in various parts of Namibia. He studied theology at the United Lutheran Seminary and Namibia Evangelical Theological Seminary in Windhoek.

Thorsten Prill *DTh, MTh, PgDipLRM, CThM, Dipl.-Volksw.*

Thorsten Prill is a Crosslinks mission partner and minister of the Rhenish Church in Namibia. He has been seconded by his church to serve as Vice-Principal at Edinburgh Bible College. Before coming to Scotland in 2017 he lectured in missiology, practical theology and systematic theology at Namibia Evangelical Theological Seminary and was involved in congregational ministry. He studied economics in Germany and theology in the UK. He holds a Doctor of Theology from the University of South Africa (UNISA).